The Art of Worldly Wisdom

THE BARNES & NOBLE LIBRARY OF ESSENTIAL READING

THE ART OF WORLDLY WISDOM

BALTASAR GRACIÁN

TRANSLATED BY MARTIN FISCHER

EDITED AND WITH AN INTRODUCTION
BY STEVEN SCHROEDER

BARNES & NOBLE
NEW YORK

THE BARNES & NOBLE
LIBRARY OF ESSENTIAL READING

Introduction, Edited Text, and Suggested Reading
© 2008 by Barnes & Noble, Inc.

Originally published in 1647

This 2008 edition published by Barnes & Noble, Inc.

Barnes & Noble, Inc.
122 Fifth Avenue
New York, NY 10011

ISBN: 978-0-7607-9106-6

Printed and bound in Canada

7 9 10 8

CONTENTS

INTRODUCTION

BALTASAR GRACIÁN'S *ART OF WORLDLY WISDOM* (1647) OFFERS PRACTICAL advice on how to make your way in a chaotic world, and how to make it well. But what sets this book apart from other manuals on the art of living is the sharp edge of the three hundred aphorisms it contains. Although Gracián wrote almost four centuries ago, the elements that describe his times bear a striking resemblance to those of our own era—political transformations, economic battles that pit local interests against global forces, competing religious outlooks seeking to shape secular worlds, and new technologies torn between democratization and centralization. Gracián wrote for an up-and-coming middle class during Spain's Golden Age, a period of transition and upheaval when new powers were emerging on the global economic and political scene. The mercantile system that now dominates the world economy was just coming into being in a political context shaped by both democratic and authoritarian tendencies. The concept of the "person" as an agent struggling for autonomy in a world of competing political and economic forces was just arising. Meanwhile, the world of arts and letters was expanding and shifting toward new forms of participation that extended beyond existing elites. Gracián's aphorisms remain relevant today as practical guides for civility in an often uncivil world. They may also serve as invitations to participate in making an uncivil world as civil as possible.

Baltasar Gracián y Morales was born in 1601 in Belmonte, near Calatayud, in Aragon, Spain. He studied at a Jesuit school in Zaragosa and became a novice at the age of eighteen. He went on to study philosophy in Calatayud and theology in Zaragosa before being ordained in 1627. Gracián joined the Society of Jesus—commonly known as the Jesuit order—in 1633 and, like many members of that order, dedicated himself to teaching and writing. He taught philosophy and theology at Jesuit schools in Aragon, Gandia, and Huesca before moving to the Jesuit College of Tarragona, He served as rector there until he was banished to the village of Graus by the Jesuit Provost General after publishing, without proper permission, the third part of his novel *El criticón* in 1657. Though some commentators imply otherwise, it is generally agreed that Gracián's transgression was not the content of the book, an allegorical journey in which civilization is contrasted with nature, so much as his failure to secure the permission of his superiors, a requirement that was routine for clergy and was particularly expected of Jesuits, whose obedience is described by the *Catholic Encyclopedia* as "the characteristic virtue of the order." Don Vincencio Juan de Lastanosa, a wealthy patron of the arts who Gracián befriended when he taught in Huesca and who was responsible for gathering the three hundred aphorisms published here (which first appeared as *Oraculo manual y arte de prudencia* in 1647), credits Gracián with twelve volumes, but only seven are known: *The Hero* (*El héroe*, 1637), a critical alternative to Machiavelli; *The Politician Don Fernando the Catholic* (*El político Don Fernando el Católico*, 1640); *Art of Ingenuity* (*Arte de ingenio*, 1642, revised as *Agudeza y arte de ingenio*, 1648); *The Complete Gentleman* (*El discreto*, 1646); and the three volumes of *The Critic* (*El criticón*, 1651–1657). These works were published under pseudonyms to avoid censorship, yet another reminder of the competing forces that complicated the task of making one's way in the world, then as now. Gracián died in Tarragona in 1658.

In the case of Spain, the "golden" of its Golden Age has to be taken literally, as the period coincides with a massive influx of gold from the territories in the so-called new world defeated and occupied by Spain beginning at the end of the fifteenth century. But the term is also meant figuratively to describe the period during the sixteenth and seventeenth centuries in which art and literature flourished throughout the Spanish Empire as the political power of the Habsburgs collapsed.

This is the period of Diego Velázquez and El Greco in art; Tomás Luis de Victoria and Alonso Lobo in music; Miguel de Cervantes, Lope de Vega, San Juan de la Cruz, and Sor Juana Inés de la Cruz in literature. And, of course, Gracián, whose *El criticón* is recognized as a masterpiece of the period and whose aphorisms were acknowledged as sources of inspiration by Goethe, Schopenhauer, and Nietzsche and influenced work such as the *Maxims* of La Rouchefoucauld. The political unification of Spain following the *Reconquista* that ended Moorish occupation and expelled or forcibly Christianized Jews, the far-flung empire that developed rapidly in the sixteenth century, and the subsequent sudden influx of wealth all contributed to cultural, economic, and political instability that created space in an Absolute State for an emerging middle class. (An earlier Jewish Golden Age depended on the Moorish occupation to make space by expelling the hostile powers that returned with the *Reconquista*.) Forces at work during the period combined contradictory impulses toward "purification" that (in writers like Bartolome de las Casas) precipitated new reflection on the nature of humanity and its relation to the inhumanity witnessed repeatedly in the course of conquest. Spain was the superpower of the age, but it was competing with steadily developing English economic and military power (as evidenced by the defeat of the Spanish Armada in 1588) as well as the power of its neighbor France.

Gracián's edge derives at least in part from the time and place in which he wrote. One important factor, noted by many critics and commentators, is the secularization of society in the previous century. Monroe Z. Hafter locates Gracián in a reaction to this secularization that he characterizes as Christian and, after 1583, anti-Machiavellian. In Hafter's reading, this reaction comes in three phases, each of which attends to divine action (and divine purpose) in the world but also takes human imperfection seriously as a given. The first phase starts with human imperfection and judges it in the light of a "rule of virtue" associated with divine purpose. It is explicitly theological and moralistic in the sense of condemning any departure from what is taken to be obedience to divine imperatives. The point is to identify sin and evoke confession. The second phase continues to take human imperfection as a point of departure while compromising on the divine imperative.

The point is to ask only as much as can reasonably be expected of imperfect human beings. It is less important to identify sin and confess than to do as much as one can in the circumstances of real human existence. The third phase is well on its way to being completely secular, proposing the "use of human means for human ends" regardless of what happens to divine purpose in the world. The point is not to deny divine purpose, but rather to bracket it as peripheral to human action, to separate *this* world from another where divine purpose rules unambiguously. In one form or another, Augustinian visions of two kingdoms were dominant by the end of the sixteenth century, and Gracián is one example of this. The effect is to move, as Hafter puts it, "from perfect to possible," leaving the perfect to the kingdom of God while discerning the possible in the various human kingdoms where we live. If politics is the art of the possible, then this third phase is decidedly political.

And Gracián is the embodiment of the third phase—certainly Christian, certainly consistent with the Jesuit outlook, and eminently practical. Gracián is quintessentially Jesuit in this regard, taking up a pragmatic Ignatian tradition that is impatient with otherworldly spirituality and committed to practical action in the world. An order that has been identified more than once as the storm troopers of the Counter-Reformation can be expected to be this-worldly—and Gracián delivers on this expectation. Like his spiritual father Ignatius, he is interested in results. And, in spite of being a critic of Machiavelli, he has a Machiavellian interest in a science of politics. Human beings are political animals, and the challenge is to make it possible for political animals to live well. So Gracián, like Machiavelli, observes human behavior in the human world and seeks to discern patterns or regularities that might become bases for laws of behavior. His close observation is part of his appeal, and it is his ability to discern and apply patterns that makes his work so durable.

Stylistically, Gracián's aphorisms have much in common with poetry. Rather than using the narrative structure of an argument to sweep readers along to a conclusion, they invite us to stop—sometimes insist that we do so—and attend to the play of words itself. Gracián delighted in language. That delight and the skill with which he pursued it have led to his acknowledgment as a literary master of the Spanish Golden Age. Some commentators have suggested that this will prove problematic for impatient modern readers, but Gracián's continued popularity suggests otherwise. His aphorisms, at least, invite reading in fits and starts rather than demanding one sustained engagement. Even if this is a trick, it may entice readers who would not take up an intricate philosophical or theological argument.

His aphoristic style is partly rooted in Jesuit practicality—a continuation of sorts of the tradition of casuistry in moral philosophy, which holds that the best way to communicate and inculcate moral principles is not by repeating them abstractly but by demonstrating their application case by case. It is partly rooted in the reaction to Machiavelli. The best way to counter a cynically practical Machiavellian political science is by developing a practically idealistic and equally scientific alternative. It is also partly rooted in a scientific tradition inherited from Hippocrates. Aphorisms are as well suited to empirically derived descriptions of particular political behaviors as to empirical descriptions of symptoms and their treatment. And in both medicine and politics, description paves the way for analysis of what works. At its best, the aphoristic style invites an experimental approach that takes it a few steps beyond proverb. An aphorism is not simply a statement of an abstract truth or an imperative. It is more properly an invitation to action—along the lines of "this has worked before, why don't you give it a try now?"

The practicality of this is particularly appealing to readers impatient with theory. For an audience confronted with a bewilderingly complex world and asking "what do we do now?" the compact form and particularity of an aphorism looks like an answer. Twenty-first-century readers who have lived with Nietzsche, Wittgenstein, and their literary offspring should know better. But even for those who know better, the appeal remains. And what carries the aphorism beyond mere proverb is its invitation. Contrary to appearances, theory is not abandoned. It is made at once provisional, implicit, and participatory. A collection of aphorisms like Gracián's is a collection of descriptions. But it is the pattern under the descriptions that gives them lasting impact; and theory is constructed on the fly in the discernment of those patterns and their application to the world. Because the world changes, the application changes; and the continuing relevance of the aphorisms depends on a community that brings the application back to the collection. Like casuistry at its best, it becomes a conversation that involves readers as equal partners with authors.

The shift from perfect to possible is paralleled by a shift from essence to appearance that contributes to Gracián's contemporary appeal. Whether or not there is some Platonic "essence" above, beyond, or behind the world, what is accessible for us in the world—and what we have to deal with in the world—is *appearance*. What one is matters less than what one is taken to be. As Gracián writes in aphorism 99, "Reality and appearance: Things do not count for what they are, but for what they seem. Few look into the depths, and many are satisfied with appearance. It is not enough to be right if it looks wrong." And so the practical question is how one can maintain some control over what one is taken to be. It is all about spin. What could be more contemporary than that?

But it would be a mistake to limit Gracián to a superficial or cynical obsession with spin alone. More properly, he is a pragmatist who has read both Niccolò di Bernardo dei Machiavelli and his increasingly Machiavellian world with care. His response to superficiality and cynicism is a critical reading that invites the kind of depth necessary to full personhood and responsible participation in human community. Cynical attention to appearances can pave the way for mere manipulation. But more critical attention to appearances may lay the foundation for an empirical description of human behavior in human worlds—and perhaps also for empirically valid participation in making worlds more human. This is clear, for example, in his attitude toward friends: "We have to live," he writes in 111, "either with friends or with enemies; so try daily to make a friend, if not a close friend, then at least someone well-disposed to you, so some may remain afterwards as confidants having passed the ordeal of selection." In the same aphorism, he says that "every friend is good," that having friends is "a second life."

Gracián understood "person" as a goal rather than a given, and his attention to appearances was directed to developing tools by which to achieve that goal. "A person who counts: You are not born so, but must strive daily to develop yourself in your person," he writes in aphorism 6, "in your calling, until perfection. The fullness of your every gift, of your every faculty. . . . Some never attain perfection, always lacking something; others are late in coming to themselves. The complete person, wise in speech, wise in action, is not just admitted, but welcomed, into that rare fellowship of those who understand." It is interesting and important that Gracián participated in creating a literary and artistic world that cultivated human autonomy and thus played a role in contributing to democratic participation. A number of critics and commentators have compared Gracián's investigation of the "person" with that of Thomas Hobbes. Hobbes distinguished "natural" from "artificial" persons and built a theory of sovereignty on the distinction. That theory of sovereignty has become the basis for seemingly contradictory visions, totalitarian and democratic. But the Hobbesian constant is a struggle, a war of each against all that is resolved provisionally and repeatedly where States and other human institutions establish sovereignty with sufficient force to hold off competitors. Gracián's attention to the imaginative exercise of autonomy in negotiating appearances highlights personal sovereignty—reasons of State for individuals. To the extent that his aphorisms are invitations rather than directives, this imaginative autonomy becomes the basis for a civil community, a community of persons.

Reading with the experience of the twentieth century behind us, it should come as no surprise that Gracián's philosophy is as susceptible as that of Hobbes or Machiavelli to totalitarian impulses. All three take up an image of struggle that makes human existence appear to be a perpetual war, and each is therefore inclined to focus on winning. That focus, of course, could partly explain the continuing appeal, since the audience that wants to win is likely to be a large one. But it also encourages an elitism that may undercut democracy. The paradoxical tension of democracy and elitism is illustrated in aphorism 133:

Better a fool with the crowd, than a sage by yourself. The politicians say that if all people are fools, no one of them can be counted such; wherefore the wise person who stands apart must be a fool. It is important, therefore, to go with the flow.

The greatest knowledge at times is to know nothing, or to affect to know nothing. We have to live with others, and the stupid make up the majority. To live alone one must have within oneself either much of God, or much of the beast: I am strongly urged to turn this aphorism about and say: Better wise with the rest of the wise, than a fool by yourself. Still some find distinction in making fools of themselves.

Gracián, more than Hobbes or Machiavelli, walks this razor edge and invites his readers to do so as well. What encourages elitism may also encourage excellence—and that is not a surprising legacy of Aristotle by way of Thomas Aquinas in a Jesuit writer.

Steven Schroeder is a poet and philosopher who lives and writes in Chicago.

THE ART OF WORLDLY WISDOM

1

Everything today has its point, but nothing is more important than becoming a person. More is required to produce one wise person today than used to be required for seven; and more is needed to deal with a single individual in these times than with an entire population in the past.

2

Mind and spirit: The two elements on which our faculties depend. One without the other is only half happiness. Mind is not enough; spirit is necessary. The fate of a fool is to fail in his calling, professional, commercial, political, social.

3

Maintain an air of uncertainty about what you do. Admiration for the new is what bestows value on the accomplished. To play with cards exposed is neither useful nor polite. Create anticipation by not declaring your purpose. And, especially where the height of your office commands public attention, display a bit of mystery about everything; and use it to further the respect in which you are held. Even when you show your hand, escape the obvious. As in everyday life, do not disclose your inner self to everyone. A prudent silence is the sacred vessel of wisdom. Purpose declared was never highly esteemed and commits itself to criticism in advance; and should it fail, the misfortune is doubled. So imitate the ways of God in order to keep those about you watchful and alert.

4

Wisdom backed by courage makes greatness. Because they are immortal, they immortalize. Each person is as great as his or her mind, and to the one who knows, everything is possible. A person without knowledge is a world in darkness. Understanding and will are the eyes and the hands; without courage, the mind is dead.

5

Create dependents: The idol is not created by the one who polishes it, but by the one who bows to it. The wise person would rather be needed than thanked. To hold people expectant is the art of the consultant; to rely upon their thankfulness is the art of the peasant: for the first remembers as the second forgets. More is to be gained from dependence than from courtesy. The person who has satisfied his thirst quickly turns his back on the well. Once squeezed, the orange changes from gold to mud. When dependence goes, reciprocity goes, and with it respect. Let this be a lesson, the first from experience: Keep hope alive but never satisfied, always remaining indispensable, even to the person in charge. But don't carry your reserve so far that your superior makes a mistake, or so far as to make the damage done by another irreversible for the sake of your personal profit.

6

A person who counts: You are not born so, but must strive daily to develop yourself in your person, in your calling, until you reach perfection. The fullness of your every gift, of your every faculty, is the goal. You will know it in the improvement of your taste, in the clarification of your thinking, in the maturity of your judgment, in the control of your will. Some never attain perfection, always lacking something; others are late in coming to themselves. The complete person, wise in speech, wise in action, is not just admitted, but welcomed, into that rare fellowship of those who understand.

7

Avoid outshining your boss. All triumph is offensive, but triumph over a superior, whether through stupidity or fate, is doubly so. Superiority has always been detested, and it is detested most thoroughly when it is greatest. With a little care, you can hide your ordinary virtues, as you might hide your beauty in casual clothes. Some will defer to you in matters of luck or of the heart. But in intelligence, no one will, certainly not a person with power. For this is the highest attribute; any attack on it is an assault on dignity. They are sovereign, and they wish to be sovereign in what is highest. They may tolerate being helped, but not surpassed. Therefore, let advice you give them appear more a jog to their memory than a beacon to what they couldn't find. The stars teach us this lesson, because, though her children are bright, they are never so forward as to outshine the sun.

8

A person who doesn't get carried away displays great loftiness of spirit. By its very superiority, such restraint redeems one from the yoke of vagrant and vulgar externals. There is no greater mastery than mastery of the self and its passions, for it amounts to the triumph of free will. But even where passion overcomes the individual, it must not dare to touch his office, especially if it be a high one. This is the best way to spare yourself grief, and yet the shortest way to a good reputation.

9

Defy the flaws of your country. As water partakes of the qualities, good or bad, of the seams through which it flows, a human being absorbs the climate of his or her birthplace. Some owe more to their country than others because a happier zenith lay above them. There is no nation, even of the most cultured, without some inborn defect which its neighbors will not at once strike upon, either for their caution or their comfort. To eradicate such national weaknesses in yourself, or at least to hide them, is a commendable skill. Thus you make yourself unique among your kind, for what is least expected is most esteemed. There are weaknesses also of race, of rank, of profession, and of age, which if gathered together in one individual and not curbed, yield an intolerable monster.

10

Fortune and fame: The one is as fleeting as the other is lasting. The first is for this life, the second for the next. The one shields against envy, the other against oblivion. Good fortune is desired and may perhaps be wheedled, but fame must be won. The wish for fame is born of quality. Fama was and is the sister of the giants; she follows only the extraordinary, either the prodigies or the monsters, that people acclaim or hate.

11

Live with those from whom you can learn. Let friendly interaction be a school for knowledge, and social contact a school for culture. To make teachers of your friends is to join the need of learning to the joy of conversation. Happiness among those who understand is mutual. They are rewarded for what they say by the approval they receive. And for what they hear, they are rewarded by what they learn. Usually it is personal interest that draws people together, but here it is glorified. A person of understanding seeks out those true aristocrats whose houses are more like stages for an heroic performance than palaces of vanity. There exist in this world people, known to the discerning, who in their bearing are true exemplars of every greatness; even the gathering of those who assist them is an academy of art and learning.

12

Nature and art: The material and the workmanship. There is no beauty unaided, no excellence that does not sink to the barbarous, unless saved by art: It redeems the bad and perfects the good. Because nature commonly forsakes us at her best, take refuge in art. The best in nature is raw without art, and the excellent is lacking if it lacks culture. Without cultivation everyone is a clown and needs polish, fine attributes notwithstanding.

13

Work toward your goals—indirectly as well as directly. Life is a struggle against human malice, in which wisdom comes to grips with the strategy of design. The latter never does what is indicated; in fact, it aims to deceive. The fanfare is in the light but the execution is in the dark, the purpose being always to mislead. Intention is revealed to divert the attention of the adversary, then it is changed to gain the end by what was unexpected. But insight is wise, wary, and waits behind its armor. Sensing always the opposite of what it was to sense and recognizing at once the real purpose of the trick, it allows every first hint to pass, lies in wait for a second, and even a third. The simulation of truth now mounts higher by glossing the deception and tries through truth itself to falsify. It changes the play in order to change the trick and makes the real appear the phantom by founding the greatest fraud upon the greatest candor. But wariness is on watch seeing clearly what is intended, covering the darkness that was clothed in light, and recognizing that design most artful which looked most artless. In such fashion, the wiliness of Python is matched against the simplicity of Apollo's penetrating rays.

14

The substance and the form: The thing does not suffice; form is also required. Bad form spoils everything, even justice and reason. Good form supplies everything, gilding the no, sweetening the truth, and perfuming decay itself. The how has much to do with things, and manners are thieves of the heart. Carrying yourself well dresses up life and pledges a happy ending to everything.

15

Hold on to clever assistants. It is the good fortune of the mighty that they can surround themselves with persons of understanding who protect them from the dangers of every ignorance, who disengage them from the snarls of every difficulty. To be served by the wise is a singular distinction, better than the barbarous taste of Tigranes, who used captive kings as servants. A new kind of leadership brings the best in life: by art to make subjects of those whom nature placed above you. Knowledge is long, but life is short; and the one who does not know, does not live. Particularly smart is the one who learns without effort and learns much from many, being taught by all. Later, in the assembly, this person speaks for the many, with the voice of all the sages he drew upon for counsel. He gains the title of oracle through the sweat of others. These superior souls first choose the lesson, then teach it later as the quintessence of wisdom. If you cannot have wisdom about you, try at least to be familiar with it.

16

Knowledge with good intentions: These two assure the happy outcome of every undertaking. A good mind combined with a bad purpose has always yielded a monster. Evil intent is the venom in every capacity. Supported by knowledge, it is a subtle poison, an unholy sovereign, that devotes itself to destruction! Science devoid of conscience is doubly insane.

17

Vary the tenor of your work. To divert attention, don't always act in the same way, especially if you are in competition. If you are always direct, they will know your course, anticipate you, and block your action. It is easy to kill a bird on the wing if it flies straight, but not if it turns. And don't always be indirect, for that trick is learned after the second feint. Malice is ever alert and much thought is necessary to outwit her. A gambler does not play the card his opponent expects, much less the one he desires.

18

Application and Minerva: Without both, no distinction; with both, distinction in the highest degree. Mediocrity gets further with application than superiority without it. Reputation is bought for the price of labor, and what has cost little is worth little. To attain even the highest posts, many have lacked only application; rarely has their talent been insufficient. To prefer to be a second in a high position to being a first in a low has good excuse. But to be satisfied with being a second in the lowest when able to be a first has none. Well, talent and art are both called for, but application seals it.

19

Do not enter where too much is anticipated. It is the misfortune of the over-celebrated that they cannot measure up to excessive expectations. The actual can never attain the imagined: for to think perfection is easy, but to embody it is most difficult. The imagination weds the wish, and together they always conjure up more than reality can furnish. For however great may be a person's virtues, they will never measure up to what was imagined. When people see themselves cheated in their extravagant anticipations, they turn more quickly to disparagement than to praise. Hope is a great falsifier of the truth; let the intelligence put her right by seeing to it that the fruit is superior to the appetite. A sound principle of faith is to excite anticipation without endangering the object of your appearance. You will make a better exit when the actual transcends the imagined, and is more than was expected. But this rule fails in the case of evil persons, for exaggeration overbuilds them too, so that when this picture is joyously reduced, what was feared as a monster of villainy comes to appear as something quite normal.

20

A person of your century: Great persons are of their time. Not all were born into a period worthy of them, and many so born failed to benefit by it. Some merited a better century, for all that is good does not always triumph. Fashions have their periods and even the greatest virtues, their styles. But the philosopher, being ageless, has one advantage: Should this not prove the right century, many to follow will.

21

The art of being lucky: There are rules to luck, for to the wise not all is accident. Try, therefore, to help luck along. Some are satisfied to stand politely before the portals of Fortuna and to await her bidding. Better are those who push forward and who employ their enterprise. On the wings of their worth and valor, they seek to embrace luck and effectively to gain her favor. And yet, properly reasoned, there is no other way to her but that of virtue and attentiveness: for none has more good luck or bad luck than wisdom or unwisdom.

22

A well-informed person: The bulwark of the prudent is noble and distinguished learning; a broad understanding of all that is happening, but in an uncommon, not common, fashion. Such persons have wit and wisdom on their tongues and they know how to use either on proper occasion: for more is often accomplished through a witty remark than through the gravest argument. And common sense has proven more valuable to many than the seven arts, however liberal they may be.

23

To be flawless: This is the requisite of perfection, yet few live without some weaknesses, either of the spirit or of the flesh. They are tormented by them when they could so easily overcome them. The critical judgment of another is always offended when some slight defect defaces a heavenly set of gifts, for a single cloud is enough to obscure the sun. Such are the shadows upon a reputation, which malice is ever quick to discover but as slow to forget. The greatest of achievements would be to transform these flaws into adornments. By such trick did Caesar know how to cover his inborn ugliness with laurel.

24

Harness the imagination: Sometimes curbing her, sometimes giving her rein, for she is the whole of happiness. She sets to rights even the understanding. She sinks to tyranny, not satisfied with mere faith, but demanding works. Thus she becomes the mistress of life itself. She does so with pleasure or with pain, according to the nonsense presented. She makes people contented or discontented with themselves. By dangling before some nothing but the specter of their eternal suffering, she becomes the scourge of these fools. To others she shows nothing but fortune and romance, while merrily laughing. Of all this she is capable if not held in check by the wisest of wills.

25

Of sound understanding: The art of arts, once, was to meditate. But this no longer suffices, for today one must be able to divine in order to escape being deceived. One cannot be understanding if one does not understand. There are diviners of the heart, and lynxes of the intent. The truths for which we most thirst are but half uttered, and only the observant gets them all. In everything that you would hear, hold a tight rein on your credulity; in everything you would not hear, use the spur.

26

Discover each person's thumbscrew. It is the way to move their will. More skill than force is required to know how to get at the heart of anyone. There is no will without its leanings, which differ as desires differ. All are idolaters: some of honor, others of greed, and most of pleasure. The trick lies in knowing these idols that are so powerful, thus knowing the impulse that moves every person. It is like having the key to another's will, with which to get at the spring within. By no means is this always one's best, but more frequently one's worst, for there are more unholy people in this world than holy. Divine a person's ruling passion, stir the person with a word, and then attack through his pet weakness: that invariably checkmates free will.

27

Rate the intensive above the extensive. The perfect does not lie in quantity, but in quality. All that is best is always scant and rare, for mass in anything cheapens it. Even among men the giants have often been true pygmies. Some judge books by their thickness, as though they had been written to exercise the arms instead of the mind. Bigness alone never gets beyond the mediocre. It is the curse of the universal man that by trying to be everything, he is nothing. It is quality that bestows distinction, in heroic proportions if the substance is sublime.

28

Be vulgar in nothing. Not in taste: Oh, how wise was the person who was downcast because his efforts found favor with the many! The hosannas of the multitude can never bring satisfaction to the discerning. Yet there exist those chameleons of popularity who find their joy, not in the sweet breath of Apollo, but in the smell of the crowd. And not in mind: Do not be taken in by what are miracles to the populace, for the ignorant do not rise above marveling. Thus the stupidity of a crowd is lost in admiration, even as the brain of an individual uncovers the trick.

29

A just person stands on the side of the right with such conviction that neither the passion of a mob nor the violence of a despot can make her overstep the bounds of reason. But who will be this Phoenix of impartiality? For justice knows few so completely dedicated to her. Many praise her, but not for themselves. Others follow her until danger threatens, and then the false deny her, and the political betray her. She pays no heed in her dealings to friendship, to power, or even to personal profit, and herein lies the danger of her disavowal. With plausible metaphysics the sly now forsake her, for they would not offend either their higher reason or the state. But a person true to herself deems such dissimulation a species of treason. Esteeming staunchness above cleverness, she finds herself wherever the truth is found, and if she changes her loyalties, it is not because of fickleness in her, but because they first changed on her.

30

Take no part in foolish enterprises, much less in schemes more likely to injure than to enhance your reputation. There exist all kinds of questionable cliques, and a thinking person flees the lot of them. There are also people of strange taste who forever marry what those wiser than them have divorced. They live well paid for their singularity, and even if they attract notice, it is more by the derision they evoke than the commendation. So the circumspect will not allow themselves to be made conspicuous even in their profession; much less, ridiculous in those matters that concern their persons. They need not be listed, for general disapprobation has sufficiently labeled them.

31

Know the lucky in order to hold to them and the unlucky in order to flee from them. Hard luck is mostly the punishment of foolishness, and no disease is so catching for the mourners. Never open the door to a small misfortune, for many more always creep in behind it, and greater ones under its protection. The great trick in cards lies in knowing what to discard: The deuce of a suit that is trump is more valuable than the ace of a suit that was. When in doubt, there is safety in sticking with the intelligent and the prudent, for sooner or later they catch up with luck.

32

Be gracious. For those who govern, it is the grand manner through which to please. It is the halo of the mighty by which they gain the goodwill of a populace. This is the single advantage of power, that it enables the holder to do more good. Those are friends who make friends. There are those, on the other hand, who can never be gracious, not so much because of peevishness but because of meanness, the very opposite in everything of the divine virtue.

33

Know how to pull back, for it is a great rule of life to know how to refuse. It becomes an even greater rule to know how to refuse yourself: either to business or to persons. There are extraneous occupations which are moths of precious time. It is worse to be busy with the trivial than to do nothing. It is not enough for the observant not to obtrude; a greater need is not to be intruded upon by others. Do not belong so wholly to others that you no longer belong to yourself. Neither exploit your friends nor ask of them more than they care to give, for everything carried to excess becomes a vice. Especially in everyday affairs, an intelligent moderation best holds goodwill and respect, for it does not bruise the so precious proprieties. Maintain therefore the freedom of your being, worship the beautiful, and do not give offense to the laws of your own good taste.

34

Know your chief asset, your great talent. Cultivate it, and help along the others. Anyone might have attained eminence in something, had he but known his advantage. Discover therefore your best attribute, and exploit it fully. Some excel in judgment, others in courage. Most violate their Minerva, and thus rise to the heights in nothing. For what is too quick in satisfying the passion is too late in pointing out its error.

35

Think, and mostly about that which is most important. All the fools get lost because they do not think; they never see the half of things. Knowing neither their loss nor their profit, they make small effort in either direction. Some make much of what is of little importance, or little of what is of much importance, always judging wrong. Most do not lose their heads because they have none. There are matters which should be considered with every faculty, and then be treasured in the depths of the mind. An intelligent person thinks about everything, though with discrimination. Such a person digs deepest where there are prospect and treasure, knowing always that more lies buried than we know. By such means, what is apprehended becomes what is comprehended.

36

Know the measure of your luck: Either to play upon it, or to get out from under it. This is far more important than to note the weather. If a person is a fool who before forty has not turned to Hippocrates for health, what greater fool is one who by this time has not turned to Seneca for wisdom. It takes great skill to manage luck: at times through patience, since there is merit in patience; at times through push, for luck has moments and moods even though they are hard to recognize, so irregular is her course. Let one who finds her propitious, strike, for luck loves the bold, as gallantry loves the young. But let one who meets her otherwise do nothing. Let that one retire lest to the bad luck prevailing there be invited more from afar.

37

Know what probing is, for it is a fine point in human intercourse. It is done to test the spirit, and by it one may with unconcern probe the most hidden and the deepest recesses of the heart. Sometimes it is malicious, sharp, poisoned with the juice of envy, and dipped in the venom of passion like unnoticed darts aimed to bring down the sublime and the estimable. Many have fallen from the favor of high or low, wounded by some trifling word, who earlier never feared a whole conspiracy of popular hatred and personal spleen. At other times it works differently, through flattery aiding and abetting the self-esteem. But with the same skill with which a plot is projected, let caution recognize it, and attentiveness expect it. Defense depends upon recognition, and the shot foreseen always misses its mark.

38

Say farewell to luck when winning: It is the way of the gamblers of reputation. Quite as important as a gallant advance is a well-planned retreat. Lock up your winnings when they are enough, or when great. Continuous luck is always suspect; more secure is that which changes. Though half bitter and half sweet, it is more satisfying even to the taste. The more luck pyramids, the greater the danger of slip and of collapse. For luck always compensates her intensity by her brevity. Fortune wearies of carrying anyone long upon her shoulders.

39

Recognize things when they are at their best, in their season, and know how to enjoy them then. The works of nature all mount to a peak of perfection; up to it they wax, beyond it they wane. Only in matters of art have a few gone to the point where they might not be improved. It is the mark of cultivated taste to enjoy everything at its best. But all may not do this, and not all who may, know how. Even the fruits of the spirit have their moment of ripeness, and it is well to recognize this, in order to value it properly and attend to it.

40

Goodwill: To gain popular admiration is much, but to gain popular affection is more. It is something that depends upon the stars, but more upon effort; for while the former give birth, the latter brings development. Great gifts are not enough even when they exist, but one easily finds the way who has found the will. So good deeds are required to engender goodwill: Do good, and do it with both hands. Be generous in speech and more generous in deed. Love in order to be loved, for true nobleness is the politic magic of the great. Turn the hand first to achievement, and then to the pen; from the blade of the sword to the blade of history. For there is such a thing as the blessing of the biographers, and it immortalizes.

41

Never exaggerate. It is a matter of great importance to forego superlatives, in part to avoid offending the truth, in part to avoid the cheapening of your judgment. Exaggeration wastes distinction and testifies to the paucity of your understanding and your taste. Praise excites anticipation and stimulates desire. Afterwards when value does not measure up to price, disappointment turns against the fraud and takes revenge by cheapening both the appraised and the appraiser. For this reason let the prudent go slowly, and err in understatement rather than overstatement. The extraordinary of every kind is always rare, wherefore temper your estimate. Exaggeration is akin to lying. Through it you jeopardize your reputation for good taste, which is much, and for good judgment, which is more.

42

Natural leadership: It is a secret strength of superiority. It never proceeds from annoying artifice but from genuine assurance. All become subject to it without knowing why, recognizing in it the hidden power of born authority. These sovereign spirits are rulers by merit, and lions by innate right. They capture the hearts and even the minds of all about them through the faith they inspire. When blessed with other gifts, they are born to be the prime movers of humankind, for they can accomplish more with one word than others with a thousand.

43

Think as the few, speak as the many. To swim against the current is just as useless for setting a matter right as it is dangerous for the swimmer. Only a Socrates may try it. To disagree with another is deemed an insult, for it is a condemnation of the other's judgment. The offended soon multiply, at times because their cause, at times because their champion, has been hurt. The truth is for the few; the false is for the populace because it is popular. A wise person cannot be recognized by what she or he says in the public square, for there the wise do not speak with their tongue, but with that of the general foolishness. By this means they better disguise their inner selves. Just so do the prudent not expose themselves to contradiction, because they do not contradict. Quick in judgment, slow in making it public. Thinking is free, and it may not be, nor can it be, strangled. Let wise persons take refuge in silence, and when at times they permit themselves to speak, let it be in the shelter of the few and the understanding.

44

A sympathy with great persons: It is the talent of the hero to agree with the hero: a veritable wonder of nature both because of its mystery and because of its usefulness. It creates a kinship of hearts and minds and its effects are such as the common ignorance attributes to love potions. It not only leads to mutual respect, but advances goodwill. It convinces without argument, and gets things done without effort. It may be active or it may be passive, but either way, it is a sublime happiness. It is a great art to recognize, to value, and to know how to attain it, for no amount of doggedness suffices without this hidden gift.

45

Be shrewd, but not too shrewd. Your reflectiveness is not something to be affected, much less detected by others. All artfulness must be concealed, for it is suspect, especially that of foresightedness, which is hated. Deceit fills the world, so be doubly suspicious without letting it be seen, for that would destroy trust in you. Suspicion vexes the spirit and cries for revenge, awakening evils of which no one dreamed. To have considered well how to proceed is of great advantage for the day's work; there is no better evidence of a person's good sense. The perfection of an undertaking lies in the masterly sureness with which it was executed.

46

Temper your antipathies. We seem to hate with pleasure, and even before we have looked. This inborn and vulgar aversion always rises against the most eminent persons. Let the intelligence overcome it, because nothing can more cheapen us than that we hate our betters. Just as sympathy with the great enhances our standing, antipathy only lowers it.

47

Avoid affairs of honor. This is the first task of prudence. Those of great capacity are not easily taxed to their limits. It takes much to drive them to one side or the other, for they always keep to the middle course of their common sense. Being slow to come to a rupture, it is much easier for them to get into something than to get out of something well. These affairs are the tempters of good sense, and it is safer to flee from them than to win through them. One matter of honor drags in another and a worse, and things are then close to the edge of downfall. There are persons who by nature, or even by nationality, are easily excited; they find it easy to involve themselves in obligations of this sort. But one who walks by the light of reason always considers carefully and will deem it braver not to become ensnarled than to win. Even the ever-present fool will opt out on the ground that one fool is enough without another.

48

A person of substance, a person who counts: There ought always to be much more on the inside than on the outside of everything. Some people are all front, like houses half-finished for lack of funds, having the entrances of a palace but the contents of a hut. There is nothing in them for which to stop or to be stopped by, because when the first greetings are over, the conversation is over. They enter to make their bows, like Sicilian horses, then go silent, for words soon fail to flow where there is no spring of thought. They take in easily those who are equally superficial; but not the intelligent, for as these look deeper and find nothing, the fiction is recognized by the discerning.

49

A person of insight and of judgment masters others rather than being mastered by them. Such a person plumbs at once the greatest depth and knows to perfection how to get at the anatomy of a soul. For such to look at someone is to see right through and understand to the core. Through uncommon observation, such a person becomes the great decipherer of that which is most deeply hidden. Looking sharply, seeing clearly, and deducing rightly, a person of insight takes in, grasps, and comprehends all that is uncovered.

50

Do nothing to make you lose respect for yourself, or to cheapen yourself in your own eyes. Let your own integrity be the standard of rectitude, and let your own dictates be stricter than the precepts of any law. Forego the unseemly, more because of this fear of yourself than for fear of the sternness of outer authority. Learn this fear of yourself, and there will then be no need for that imaginary monitor of Seneca.

51

A person of discernment: Most of life is discernment; it calls for good taste and the best of judgment, for neither learning nor mind is enough. There is nothing perfect where there is not choice. Two qualities are required: the power to choose, and the power to choose the better. And yet in this, many with creative minds, sharp understanding, learning, and experience still fail. Forever consorting with the worse, it is as though they are determined to go wrong. So discernment comes to be one of the greatest gifts from on high.

52

Never lose your head. It is a matter of great practical wisdom never to let it get away from you: Composure marks the great person of noble heart, for all greatness is hard to throw off balance. The passions are the humors of the spirit, and their every excess makes the mind sick. And if the disease escapes through the mouth, it endangers the reputation. Wherefore have such mastery over self, and be so strong, that nothing, either in the greatest fortune or in the greatest adversity, can upset you, remaining superior even to the admiration of this feat.

53

Diligent and intelligent: Diligence quickly accomplishes what the intelligence has well thought out. Haste is the passion of fools. Since they don't know the difficulties, they work without heed. Wiser persons, on the other hand, are likely to fail from overcaution, for reflection breeds delay. Their hesitation in acting loses them the fruits of their good judgment. Promptitude is the mother of fortune. One does much who leaves nothing for tomorrow. A magnificent motto: Make haste slowly.

54

Have strength of spirit. A lion is dead if even the rabbits pull its hair, for there is no sneering at courage. If concession is made in one instance, it will have to be made in a second, and so on even to the last. The same effort required to win late would have availed more if expended earlier. Courage of the spirit is more than courage of the body. It is like a sword sheathed in the scabbard of your heart, ready for the occasion. It is the protector of your person: but more against the hurt of its soul than the hurt of its flesh. Many have been rich in mind, but because they were poor in this courage of the spirit, they lived as the dead, and died for what they lacked. For it is not without plan that nature has joined the sweetness of the honey with the sharpness of the sting in the bee. Nerves and bones make up the body; don't allow its spirit to be all softness.

55

A person who can wait: It marks a great heart, endowed with patience, never to be in undue haste or excited. Be first the master of yourself, and then you will be the master of others. One must journey far through time to get to the core of anything. A prudent waiting brings season to accomplishment and ripeness to what is hidden. The crutch of time accomplishes more than the iron club of Hercules. Even God does not tame with a whip, but with time. A great truth this: Time, and I against any two. Fortune herself crowns patience with the grandest of garlands.

56

Have good impulses. They are the fruit of a fortunate quickness. Fearing neither hazard nor accident because of their faith in their own vitality and alertness, some think long only to go wrong in everything afterwards. Others succeed in everything without ever having thought before. They are veritable machines which function best when under strain. They are freaks who when pushed, succeed at everything, but given time, at nothing. What does not come to them at once never comes, for there is nothing to which they may appeal afterwards. The quick are always well received because their very appearance argues capacity: of their minds by their alertness, and of their labors by their spirit.

57

That done with deliberation is done quickly enough, and better. What is made in haste is unmade as quickly. What is to last an eternity may well take another to create. Nothing arrests the attention unless it is perfect, and perfection alone makes accomplishment eternal. The mind that has profundity attains immortality. That which is worth most has also cost most. Even the most precious of the metals is that which is heaviest and slowest to melt.

58

Know how to vary your front. Do not show yourself the same way to everybody, and do not expend more energy than is needed. Waste nothing, either of knowledge or of strength: A good falconer does not loose more birds than suffice to get the game. Do not put everything into the showcase at once, or none will pause to admire on another day. Always keep something new in reserve with which to dazzle tomorrow, for one who uncovers something fresh each day maintains the interest and never allows another to discover the limits of his treasure.

59

Make a good exit. One who enters the house of fortune through the gate of pleasure leaves it through the gate of sorrow. Keep the curtain in mind, paying greater attention to the happy exit than to the applauded entrance. It is the fate of the unlucky to be off to a happy start and a tragic finish. There is no point to the applause of the vulgar on appearance, for everybody gets it. But there is, to the feeling which remains on exit, for those encored are rare. Fortune follows few as they leave; polite as she is to the arriving, she is equally rude to the departing.

60

Good judgment: Some are born wise, with an inborn sense of right and wrong. Entering upon a prudent conduct of life, thus half their journey to success is over. The years and experience develop their understanding, and so they attain a judgment most tempered. They despise all prejudice as a temptation of the spirit: especially in matters of state which, because of their great importance, demand absolute uprightness. They deserve to have direction of the ship of state, either to steer it or to lay its course.

61

Preeminence in what is best: Strive to be the best of all perfections. There is no chance to be the hero if not possessed of some sublime attribute. Mediocrities are not the subjects of applause. Only eminence in a high calling cuts a person out of the common herd and into the class of the rare. To be excellent in a humble calling is to be something, but in something small. It may carry much of what brings delight but only little of what brings fame. To be excellent in great things is to assume the character of a sovereign; it evokes admiration, and it gains goodwill.

62

Work with good tools. Some seek to exhibit their cleverness by pointing to the poor qualities of their tools: a dangerous type of self-satisfaction to be followed by stiff punishment. The excellence of a servant has never dulled the splendor of the master. All the glory of what is accomplished later descends upon the first cause, as, in reverse, all the disgrace. Fame walks only with principals. She never says: This one had a good subordinate and that one, a bad. But only: This one did well, and that one did poorly. Hence, choose well and make study, for on that depends the immortality of your reputation.

63

Excellent, to be first in any line, and doubly excellent if the line is great: A big advantage to be the player of the hand if the deal has been fair. Many a person might have been a Phoenix at her job had there

not been others before her. The first in any line are crowned innova-
tors by fame. The rest must beg their bread, for however much they
sweat, they cannot rid themselves of the vulgar charge of imitation.
The mark of the extraordinary is to have blazed new trails to glory, and
in such fashion that the intelligence assured the success of the enterprise from the start. By the mere business of being the first in any
undertaking wise persons have made a place for themselves in the
roster of the heroic. For which reason some have preferred to be firsts
in a second class to being seconds in a first.

64

Know how to escape grief. A profitable maxim, for it is the way to
escape regret. A little prudence helps much, for she is the light of
happiness and therefore of peace. Don't be the purveyor of scandal
or its recipient, but forbid it entrance, much less give it aid. One person keeps his ears only to have them bathed in sweet flattery; another,
only to have them deafened by the bitterness of evil gossip. For there
are those who cannot live without some daily dirt, as Mirthridates
could not without his poison. Neither is it the law of self-preservation
that you must wish upon yourself a lifelong regret, in order to provide
momentary pleasure to another, however close to you. Never sin
against your own happiness in order to comfort another who comes
for advice and then does not stay. In every situation which spells joy
to another and pain to you, this is the proper rule. It is better that he
be downcast today than that you be tomorrow, and helpless in the
matter to boot.

65

Of cultivated taste: It can be cultivated as intelligence can be cultivated. The better the appreciation, the greater the appetite, and
when fulfilled, the greater the enjoyment. Greatness of spirit is
known by the richness of the things needed to gratify it. For it takes
much to satisfy a great capacity. Just as much food is required for
large hunger, even so does the sublime in spirit demand the sublime
in matter. The boldest objects of nature fear this judgment of taste,
and the finest in art trembles before it. Few are the stars of the first

magnitude; let appreciation of them be equally choice. Taste and contact have a way of going together, and the inheritance is in line. It is a great good fortune to consort with those who have taste at its best. But neither should a trade be made of dissatisfaction with everything. That is the extreme of fools, and odious in proportion to its affectation and its intemperateness. Some would wish God to create another world, and of wholly different ideals, in order to satisfy their crazy fantasies.

66

Keep the happy ending in mind. Many lay greater stress upon the rules in the way to an end than upon the happy attainment of that end. Yet the shame of failure has always outweighed any approbation of the pains taken in accomplishments. The winner does not have to explain. Most see nothing of the means to an end, but only the good or the bad outcome. So one who accomplishes his end does not endanger his reputation. A happy finish makes everything shine, no matter how unfitting the means may have been. Which explains why at times it should be the rule to offend the rules when it is not possible by other methods to attain a happy ending.

67

Choose an occupation that brings distinction. Most things depend upon the satisfaction they give others. Appreciation is to talent what the west wind is to the flowers: breath and life itself. There are occupations which enjoy public acclaim, and there are others, even though more important, which receive no recognition. The former, because done in the sight of everybody, win popular favor. The latter, even though they possess more of the rare and the worthy, remain unnoticed because done in obscurity. They may be venerated, but they receive no approbation. Among princes, it is the victorious who are celebrated. It is for this reason that the kings of Aragon are so highly honored as warriors, conquerors, and great men. Let the man of gifts find himself a place thus prized, where all may see him and all may play a part with him. Then will the voice of the people hold him immortal.

68

To jog the understanding is a greater feat than to jog the memory: For it takes more to make a person think than to make one remember. Some fail to strike when the iron is hot because they fail to see the opportunity; so let a bit of friendly advice help them to see their chance. One of the great attributes of the mind is its power to know when opportunity offers. But where such mind is lacking, many things fail to be done which might have been. On which account let the one give light who has it, and let the one seek it who needs to: the former with reserve, the latter with ardor. But let it not be more than mere suggestion. Such reticence is necessary, and in proportion to the stake involved of the one who makes it. Show your interest and go beyond it but not too far: If you receive a no, go in search of a yes. But do so with art, for in most instances nothing is won because nothing was ventured.

69

No slave to vulgar moods: A great person is never the victim of passing fancies. This is a good precept to meditate upon yourself, to discover your present mood and to prepare against it. Or even to throw yourself into an opposite one, in order to come to rest between the natural and the assumed, on the balance point of common sense. It is a first principle that in order to improve yourself, you must first know yourself. For there exist veritable monsters of moodiness, always of a different temper, and of a different mind with each. Eternally enslaved by their smug intemperance, they involve themselves most consistently, their excess checkmating not only their purpose but attacking their judgment, thus defeating both their ends and their plan.

70

Know how to say no. You cannot say yes to everything or to everybody, so it is important to know how not to say yes. This is especially vital in those who command, for here fashion enters. The no of one person is more esteemed than the yes of another, for a no that is embellished may be more satisfying than a yes unembellished. There are many who carry an eternal no in the mouth with which they spoil everything. It always comes first, so that even when later they grant everything, such answer gives little satisfaction because of the bad taste provided by the first. Refusal should never be flat, the truth appearing by degrees. Nor should it be absolute, for that would cancel dependence, so some remnant of hope must be kept alive to sweeten the bitterness of the refusal. Employ courtesy to fill the void of the denial, and let pleasing words disguise the failure of action. Yes and no are quickly spoken, but they demand long consideration.

71

Not eccentric: Not freakish in manner, either by nature or by affectation. A thinking person is ever the same in all he does, for upon this is founded his reputation as a person of wisdom. Change in him depends upon himself and has its causes and its reasons; in matters of common sense mere moodiness is something abhorrent. There are those who are of different face daily, until even their judgment goes awry. In like proportion goes their will, and so even, their luck. What was yesterday the white of their yes is today the black of their no. Always ruining the good opinion, they fog the concept people had of them.

72

A person of decision: Poor execution is not as bad as indecision, for matter in motion does not rot like stagnant matter. Some are so incapable of decision that they need constantly to be prodded from without. This springs at times less from a confused judgment, since theirs may be unusually clear, than from unwillingness to act. It is an evidence of genius to foresee difficulties, but an evidence of greater genius to be able to see the way out of such difficulties. Others are embarrassed by nothing, and possessed as they are of great judgment and determination, they are born for the highest posts. Because their quick comprehension eases the day's business and speeds it, whatever they tackle is soon finished. After having set one world in order, time is left to start upon another, and inasmuch as they feel that luck is with them, they set forth in confidence.

73

Know the meaning of evasion. It is the prudent person's way of keeping out of trouble. With the gallantry of a witty remark one is able to extricate oneself from the most intricate of labyrinths, to emerge gracefully from the bitterest encounter and with a smile. It was to this that the greatest of the great captains ascribed his power. A courteous way of saying no is to change the conversation, nor is there greater politeness than that of not being able to understand.

74

Not unapproachable: It is in the government that the really ungoverned have their being. To be unapproachable is the vice of people who do not know themselves; they confuse their spleen with their splendor. The road to affection does not lie in surliness. A show indeed, one of these erratics, making a point of his exclusiveness! His unfortunate subordinates enter to have speech as to battle with a tiger, as full of spears as of fears. To win office, such a person could get himself in with everybody. But having arrived, his presumptuousness gets him out with everybody. Because of his place he should be accessible to the many. But because of his gall or his spite, he becomes accessible to none. A just punishment, to let him be, robbing him of both his brains and his following.

75

Choose a heroic ideal, more as something to emulate than as something to imitate. Examples of greatness lie about us, living texts of renown. Let each set before himself the greatest in his line, not so much as something to follow as something to spur him on. Alexander did not weep over Achilles dead, but over himself unborn, as yet, to glory. There is nothing that so thrills the ambition as the clarion of another's fame. For that same impulse which buries jealousy lifts up the noble spirit.

76

Not the jester always: The common sense of a person is found in his seriousness, for wisdom ranks higher than wit. One who is always the buffoon is really never the man. He classes himself with the liar, in that neither is believed: not the latter, because his word is doubted, and not the former, because of his scoffing. For it is never known if what was said was weighed in the mind, which in no instance can have been much. There is nothing more banal than continuous banter. Thus some get the reputation of being witty, but they endanger thereby their reputation of being wise. The humorous may be allowed its moment, but for all the rest, the serious.

77

Know how to be all things to all people. A wise Proteus, one who is learned with the learned, and with the pious, pious. It is the great way of winning all to you: for to be like is to be liked. Observe each person's spirit and adapt yourself to the serious or to the jovial, as the case may be, by following the fashion through a politic change within yourself. This is a veritable necessity in those who are dependent. But this great rule of life calls for rich talent. It is least difficult to that worldly person whose mind is filled with knowledge and whose spirit is filled with taste.

78

Art in execution: Fools always rush in, for all fools are rash. Their very simplicity, which at the start makes them insensible to advice, at the finish makes them insensible to disgrace. But the wise enter with great care; their bodyguards are watchfulness and caution. These scout out the hidden, so that progress may be made without danger. To dash in regardless stands condemned by discretion as foolhardy, even though luck at times absolves the venturer. Go slowly where the shoals are many. Let foresight feel the way, and let caution determine the ground. There are today great shallows in the human sea, so proceed always with the leadline.

79

Of happy mind: In moderation, it is an asset and not a liability. A bit of humor seasons everything. The greatest man plays the fool at times, for it makes him popular. But his manners are forever checked by his mind, and proper homage is paid to decorum. Some can make of a bit of wit a shortcut out of every difficulty. Certain things should be taken lightly; often they are the very ones which others take most seriously. He who shows himself affable captures all hearts.

80

Alert when seeking information: We live for the most part by what is told us; there is little that we see. We live in the faith of others. The ear is the side door of truth, but the front door of falsehood. The truth is sometimes seen, but rarely heard. On the fewest of occasions does it arrive in its elemental purity, especially if it has traveled far, for then it is always soiled by what has happened on the road. Feeling tinges with her colors all that she touches, sometimes happily, sometimes unhappily. She always leaves some kind of mark. So listen cautiously to the admirer, more cautiously to the informer. It requires the whole attention at such times to discover the intent of the newsbearer, in order to know beforehand which foot he is going to put forward. With reflection look into what may be foolish and what may be false.

81

Know how to renew your glitter. It is the birthright of the Phoenix. Even the best goes stale, and so its fame. Familiarity kills admiration, so something fresh, though mediocre, comes to outshine the greater virtue, grown old. Bring about, therefore, your rebirth in courage, in spirit, in fortune, in everything. Clothe yourself anew in shining armor and rise again like the sun. Change the theater for your appearance, in order that your absence from the one may evoke desire, and your novelty in the other, applause.

82

Drink nothing to the dregs, either of the bad or of the good, for to moderation in everything has one sage reduced all wisdom. Too great justice becomes injustice, and the orange, squeezed too hard, turns bitter. Even in enjoyment, do not go too far. The spirit itself grows weary if worked too long, and one who milks too hard draws blood instead of milk.

83

Allow yourself some pardonable defect, for a certain weakness at times may be the greatest evidence of strength. Envy carries its ostracisms, as civil as they are criminal. It accuses the most holy of sin, because without sin, and because totally perfect, condemns totally. Envy makes of itself an Argus to discover the flaws of the flawless for its own comfort. Detraction, like lightning, only strikes the greatest heights. At such times, therefore, let Homer sleep, and let him affect some lack of spirit or of virtue, but not of prudence. In order to appease envy, so it does not burst of its own poison, wave a cloak before the bull of jealousy to rescue immortality.

84

Know how to profit through your enemies. Learn how to grasp a thing, not by its blade which cuts, but by its hilt which protects, especially in the battle of life. A wise person's enemies are of more use to her than a fool's friends. Evil intent often levels a mountain of difficulty which the best intent in the world could not hope to climb over. Many have been made through the greatness of their enemies. Flattery is to be feared more than hate, since this exposes the flaws which flattery would conceal. The person who knows makes a mirror of spite, more faithful than the mirror of affection, and envisages her shortcomings to correct them. For prudence grows apace when it must live against rivalry or malevolence.

85

Do not be the ace. The fault of all that is best is that its overuse comes to be its misuse. The cry of all for it comes to be the cry of all against it. To be good for nothing is a great misfortune; not a lesser is to be good for everything. Such persons end losers in spite of all they win, and live to be as despised as once they were desired. The aces of every kind become dog-eared through overplay. Having fallen from the high estimation in which once they were held, they are consigned to the class of the common. The one protection against either extreme is to hold to a middle place in the limelight, letting the superb in you reside in your qualifications and not in your show of them. The brighter the torch, the quicker its burning, and the sooner its end. The fewer the performances, the higher the price paid for admission.

86

Avoid evil gossip. The mob has many heads, and thus many eyes for malice and many tongues for slander. Let it start to gossip and the greatest reputation is sullied. Let it develop a catchword and an honored name is blotted out. The thing commonly starts from some visible defect, in some ridiculous weakness, that lends itself easily to a tale. And sometimes it is the prying malice of a rival that feeds the mob; for there are hissers of malevolence, and they demolish a reputation most quickly with a jeer and a gibe. It is easy to give a person an evil name, because evil is gladly believed, but it takes much to blot it out. Wherefore the person of intelligence guards himself against such accident by pitting his caution against the popular insolence. For it is easier to keep out, than to get out of trouble.

87

Culture and polish: Every human being is born a barbarian, and only culture redeems them from the bestial. Culture makes the person, the more the better. In this faith Greece could call the rest of the world barbarous. Ignorance is rough, and nothing refines more than learning. But even this learning remains a crude affair if sloven. Not only does our understanding require polish, but our desires as well, and especially our conduct. Some people are naturally polished, noble within and without, in thought and speech, and in bodily dress, which may be compared to the bark of a tree, as their gifts of the spirit may be likened to its fruit. Others are as naturally unpolished, so that all they have, even to their good points, seems eternally soiled by something unbearable.

88

Generous in action to secure sublimity in it: The great person may not be small in his actions. He must not draw too fine distinctions, least of all in trivial matters. Even though it is well to take in everything, it is not so well to seem to peer into everything. Go at the day's work in

that large spirit which is the mark of gallantry. The great law in government is tolerance; most things should be allowed to pass unnoticed
between intimates, between friends, and particularly between enemies. All stickling is a vexation of the spirit and a burden to the soul.
To return time after time to the same annoyance is a sort of insanity.
And so the way in which a person deports himself is very likely to be
the measure of his heart and his mind.

89

A realistic assessment of yourself: Of your spirit, of your mind, of
your judgment, of your passion. No one can be master of himself who
does not first understand himself. There are mirrors for the face, but
none for the soul. So make one out of careful consideration of yourself. And while it may be well to forget the outer image, remember
the inner in order to fill out its defects, to make it better. Poll the
powers of your mind and of your will in order to achieve something. Take stock of what temper you have for the business of the day.
Sound your depths, and measure your capacity for everything.

90

The art of living fully, of living well: Two are done quickly with life: the
fool and the dissolute. The one as a result of not knowing how to pre-
serve it, and the other as a result of not knowing its value. As virtue is
its own reward, so vice is its own punishment. One who lives too fast
is finished quickly and in a double sense, while one who rests in virtue
never dies. For the life of the spirit becomes the life of the body, and
the life lived well gathers both length and fullness of days.

91

Always proceed without misgivings. The mere fear of failure in the one
acting is already its certainty in the observer, especially if the observer
is a rival. If judgment had its doubts even in the heat of passion, later,
when freed from such passion, it will condemn the whole enterprise
and declare it stupid. Every undertaking of which you question the
prudence is dangerous, and safety lies in leaving it alone. Wisdom
does not debate possibilities; it walks only in the noonday light of the
intelligence. How can any venture come off well which even in its

conception was questioned by reason? And if plans unanimously passed by our very souls have a way of ending unhappily, what may be expected of those conceived by a hesitant mind and thought bad by the judgment?

92

Expansive intelligence I say, in everything: It is the first and the greatest rule in work and in speech, particularly for those who occupy the most important and highest offices. One grain of common sense is of larger weight than a bushel of cunning. It is the high road to peace, though not so filled with cheers. Even if the reputation of being wise is the triumph of fame, it is enough to have satisfied those who have understanding. Their judgment is the touchstone of what is well done.

93

A whole person: To be a person of many facets is to count as many persons. Such a person makes life richer by bestowing his wealth upon his neighborhood. Variety in what is best is the joy of life. A great art, that of knowing how to garner all that is good. Since nature has made in humans an epitome of herself by giving them highest standing, let art make each person into a little universe through the exercise and the development of taste and of mind.

94

Immeasurable capacity: A watchful person will decline to be plumbed to the depths, whether of knowledge or of capacity. If one would remain esteemed, let him allow himself to be known, but not to the point of being comprehended. Permit no one to discover the limits of your capacities, because of the obvious danger of disillusionment. Never allow another to see through you completely. Surmise and supposition regarding the talents of any person win greater respect than definite knowledge, no matter how great they be.

95

Know how to keep anticipation alive. Always strive to feed it by letting much promise more. Allow one achievement to be only the announcement of a greater one. Don't put all your reserves into the first throw.

The great trick is to dole out strength, and to dole out mind, in such fashion as to bring forward bit by bit the fulfillment of what was expected of you.

96

An expansive rule of conscience: It is the shrine of reason and the foundation of prudence. Its faith makes easy the attainment of every goal. It is a gift from heaven, and the most to be desired because heaven's first and greatest. It is the very breastplate of armor, and so much so, that nothing else a man may lack will allow him to be called not a man, but only a richer or poorer one. All the activities of life depend upon its influence, and all beg its good opinion. Everything must pass in judgment before it. It consists of an inborn love for all that conforms most to reason, marrying always with that which is most true.

97

Attain and maintain a reputation. It is a property of fame that does not belong to you but is available for your use. It is a stiff climb, because it is a child of eminence, as rare as mediocrity is common. But once attained, it is easily maintained. It asks for much, but it yields more. When it rises to the height of veneration, it becomes majestic, either because of the sublimity of its cause or of its influence. But only the well-founded reputation endures.

98

Hide your purpose. The passions are windows of the soul. And practical wisdom calls for acting. To play with cards exposed is to risk defeat. Pit the defense of caution against the offense of the adversary: against the eye of the lynx, the ink of the cuttlefish. Even our wishes must not be voiced, so that they may not be met, by the one to deny them or by another to satisfy them.

99

Reality and appearance: Things do not count for what they are, but for what they seem. Few look into the depths, and many are satisfied with appearance. It is not enough to be right if it looks wrong.

100

An unbiased person, a thinking Christian: A worldly philosopher who does not appear, much less affect to be such. Philosophy stands discredited today, even though it was once the major pursuit of the sages. The science of the thinker lives degraded. Seneca introduced it into Rome; it found favor for a time in the courts, but today it is reckoned nonsense. And yet the detection of error was always the food of the thinking spirit and the joy of the righteous.

101

Half the world laughs at the other half, though all are fools. Either everything is good or everything is bad, depending on the vote. What one sues, another pursues. An insufferable fool, he who wishes the universe regulated according to his plans. Bliss does not derive from the pleasure of any one person. There are as many minds as there are heads, and as different. There is no weakness without its admirer. Don't worry that your ways displease some, because, without fail, they will please others. And don't let their approval of them go to your head, because still others will condemn them. Proper satisfaction may be taken only in the approval of persons of authority and those who have standing in their fields. Do not live by the sanction of any one voice, or of any one custom, or of any single period.

102

A stomach for great slabs of fortune: In the body of wisdom, a big mouth is an organ of no minor importance, because great capacity requires large portions. One worthy of more will not be gorged by good fortune. One person's indigestion is another's appetite. Many get sick when the food is rich, because they are naturally weak. They are neither accustomed to nor born to high living. The business sours on them, and they get dizzy on the fumes of their unearned distinction. They run great danger in their high places, unable to maintain themselves in them because unaccustomed. So let the really big person display the capacity for even larger enterprise, and scrupulously avoid anything that suggests a faint heart.

103

Everyone majestic, after a fashion: Every man's actions should be fit
for a king, regal within the limits of his gifts. Greatness in action and
loftiness of mind in everything done mark the king by merit, if not
by birth. True sovereignty lies in perfection of conduct. No need for
a king to begrudge another a grandeur of which he is the prototype.
Especially in those appointed to the throne, something of this truly
sovereign quality should stick to them. Only let them not merely
assume the attributes of majesty in vain ceremony and grow pompous,
but let them realize these within themselves.

104

Take the pulse of every position. There is variety to them, and you
need the mind of a judge to know their values; yet nothing calls for
greater care in choice. Some demand courage, and others shrewdness.
It is most easy to manage in those which call merely for honesty, and
most difficult in those which call for skill. With decent endowment,
nothing else is necessary for the former. But for the latter, attention
and sleeplessness may not suffice. It is a tiring task to govern human
beings, most of whom are crazy or stupid: Double brains are needed
with those who have none. Most intolerable are those posts which
require the whole of a person for set hours and at set tasks. Better are
those freer from weariness that join the serious to variety, because
change refreshes the spirit. Most to be desired are those that carry a
measure of independence. Worst are those which sweat a person to
death in human, but also in divine terms.

105

Not a bore: The person of one deal or of one speech is dull. Brevity
charms, and it is better business. It makes up in manner what it lacks
in measure. The good, if short, is doubly good. Even the bad, if brief,
is not so bad. The essence is always stronger than a hodgepodge. It is
common knowledge that the long-winded person is rarely wise, either
in the material at hand or in the form of the discourse. There are
people who burden the world more than they adorn it, mere tinsel
that everybody pushes aside. A person of discernment will avoid being

a nuisance, especially to important people who are busy. It is worse to annoy anyone of them than the rest of the world put together. What is well said is said quickly.

106

Don't make a show of wealth. It is more offensive to show off your position than your person. To make yourself the central figure is to invite envy. The harder you pursue deference, the less likely you are to get it. Respect depends on others; one cannot snatch it, only deserve it and wait. Big jobs demand distinction in their exercise, without which they are not worthily administered. So maintain in them the dignity necessary to the proper discharge of their obligations, not insisting on respect, but earning it. For all who trade upon their offices show that they do not merit them, and that they are not big enough for the honor. If you would be important, let it be through the excellence of your talents rather than through your position. Even a king should be honored more because of his qualifications than because of the accident of his birth.

107

No displays of self-satisfaction: Be neither discontented, for that is cowardice, nor self-satisfied, for that is stupidity. Self-complacency starts for the most part in witlessness. It ends in a blissful ignorance which even though soothing to the soul, is not to your credit. Because unable to equal the great qualifications of another, you are content with some vulgar mediocrity within yourself. It is always more useful and more intelligent to have misgivings about yourself: either for your better assurance that things will come off well, or for your better comfort if they come off badly. One cannot be surprised by a turn of luck who has already anticipated it. Even Homer has to sleep, and Alexander has to come down from his pedestal and out of his delusion. Things depend upon many circumstances, and what was a triumph in one place on one occasion becomes a disgrace in another. But what is most unruly about this form of stupidity is that complacency flowers and then pops up everywhere from its seeds.

108

The shortest road to being a person: Know whom to follow. Contact is the most effective way in which to learn manner and taste. One thus takes on the thought and even the spirit of others without being aware of it. Let the intemperate, therefore, join up with those more temperate; and so with the rest of the mental attributes, that the person of moderation may be brought forth without violence. A great trick is to know how to adapt yourself. The play of contrasts makes this universe beautiful and sustains her. And if it will bring about such harmony in the physical world, it will accomplish an even greater harmony in the moral world. Avail yourself of this courteous admonition in the choice of your friends and associates, so that through the meetings of the extremes there may arise a most sensible mean.

109

Don't be accusing. There are evil-minded people who would make everything a crime, not because they care but because they can. They condemn everybody: some for what they have done, others for what they may do. It is the sign of a narrow mind, as cruel as it is vile, for they charge so immoderately that of specks they fashion beams with which to put out the eyes. Slave drivers in every position, they would make a galley of what was an elysium. In the midst of excitement, they push everything to extremes. The large soul, on the other hand, finds an excuse for everything, if not in intention then in inattention.

110

Do not wait to be the sun in her setting. It is a maxim of the wise to leave before being left. Know how to make a triumph even of your exit. At times the sun herself when most bright will retire behind a cloud, that she may not be seen to sink. Thus she leaves us in doubt as to whether or not she has set. Escape such accident in order not to suffer slight; do not wait until people turn their backs on you, burying you alive in your feelings, but dead in their estimation. The person of foresight puts his horse in the stable when the time is right and does not wait to see it create laughter by falling in the middle of the race. The beauty wisely cracks her mirror when it is yet early, not later with impatience when it has disillusioned her.

111

Have friends. It is a second life. Every friend is good and wise to a friend. Between them everything comes off well. A person's value is determined by others, and to have great value, one must find the way to their hearts. There is no magic like that of friendly service. The best way to have friends is to make friends. The most and the best of what is ours depends upon others. We have to live either with friends or with enemies; so try daily to make a friend, if not a close friend, then at least someone well-disposed to you, so some may remain afterwards as confidants having passed the ordeal of selection.

112

Gain goodwill, for even the first and highest includes it and gives it place. Through it is won a favorable disposition. Some have such faith in its virtue that they hold diligence cheap. The alert know well that the path of mere merit is stony if one is not helped along by goodwill. It eases and aids everything, not always supposing the existence of great virtues like courage, honesty, learning and even conscience, but imposing them. It fails to see all shortcomings, because it does not wish to see them. Ordinarily it springs from mere similarity in material interests, as those of the body, the nation, the family, the country or the profession. But in its deeper form it is more noble, having to do with the talents, character, fame, and merit. All the difficulty lies in arousing goodwill, for its maintenance is easy. But goodwill can be won, and its power should be known.

113

Prepare yourself in good fortune for the bad. It is expedient in the summer to make provision for the winter, and much more convenient. At that time goodwill comes cheap, and friends are plentiful. It is good then to garner the two against bad times when adversity shows her face and all things fail. Gather up your friends and those beholden to you, for someday you may appreciate what you do not need today. The evil have no friends in their prosperity because they do not know them, and in their adversity because they are not known by them.

114

Never compete. Every effort to outshine an opponent lowers your standing, for competition resorts at once to mudslinging in order to besmirch. They are few who carry on war in fair fashion, for rivalry lays bare the flaws which courtesy has covered over. Many lived in honor as long as they had no emulators. The heat of combat calls up and brings to life infamies long dead, and digs up stenches forgotten. Competition starts with a manifesto of slander and calls to its aid whatever it can, not what it should. When at times—most of the time—insults turn out to be the wrong weapons for victory, these people find a vile satisfaction in their spite. They bandy it about with so much air that the dust of forgetfulness is shaken from old scandals. People of goodwill have always been people of peace, and people of honor, people of goodwill.

115

Accustom yourself to the defects of those about you, as you would accustom yourself to an ugly face. This is the best way out when you are a subordinate, for there are beasts no one can live with and no one can live without. It is therefore the part of wisdom to get used to them as to ugliness itself, in order that on some terrible occasion you may not forget yourself. When first seen they terrify, but little by little this fear grows less. Reflection hardens against the unpleasant or learns how to bear it.

116

Always deal with honorable people. With such only may you be involved, and such only may you involve. What they have done is best pledge of what they will do, even in the business of shuffling the cards. For they deal aboveboard, and so it avails more to lose with people of honor than to win with those of dishonor. There is no profit in crookedness, because it is unbeholden to honesty. On this

account there is no true friendship among thieves; nor are their pro-
testations of friendship true, even when they seem it, for they are
not made in good faith. Those without honor should be shunned,
for they who do not cherish honor do not cherish virtue, and honor
is the throne of virtue.

117

Never talk about yourself. Either you praise, which is vanity, or you
reproach, which is poor spirit. Both evince a guilty heart in the
speaker, which gives pain to the listener. If it is to be avoided in private
life, it is to be shunned even more in public office where you speak to
the crowd, and where you look like a fool if you give even a hint of it.
A similar weakness of mind lies in speech about those present, because
of the danger of foundering on either of two rocks: that of overappre-
ciation or that of disparagement.

118

Gain a reputation for courtesy and you will be loved. Courtesy is the
key ingredient of culture, a kind of sorcery that gains everyone's affection, just as discourtesy merits scorn and universal hatred. When
discourtesy is born of arrogance, it is abominable; when of coarseness,
detestable. More rather than less, but never equal, lest courtesy degenerate into injustice. Hold to it as a matter of duty between enemies, for
it shows your courage, costing little and being worth much. To show
honor is to be honored. Gallantry and honor have this advantage:
They are saved through being spent, the first if practiced, the second
if worn.

119

Do not make yourself hated. Do not provoke aversion. It will come
quickly enough without invitation. There are many who hate gratis,
without knowing why or wherefore. Ill will has a way of outdistancting
goodwill, for the urge in us to injure another is more potent and
swifter than the desire to advantage ourselves. Some are happy only
when at outs with everybody, either because vexed, or to vex. When
hate has once taken hold of a person, it is as hard to get rid of as a

bad reputation. People of clear judgment are feared, the evil-tongued are abhorred, the presumptuous make sick, the buffoons are detested, and the singular are left to themselves. Try, therefore, to show appreciation in order to be appreciated, and let anyone who desires affection show affection.

120

Live according to custom. Even wisdom must be in style, and where it is not, it is well to know how to feign ignorance. Thought and taste change with the times: Do not be old-fashioned in thought and modern in taste. The choice of the many carries the vote in every field. For the time being, therefore, it must be bowed to, in order to bring it to a higher level. The person of wisdom accommodates to the present, even though the past seems better, alike in the dress of his spirit as in the dress of his body. Only in the matter of being decent does this rule of life not apply, for virtue should be practiced eternally. Yet today it is unknown, and to speak the truth and to keep one's word seem the marks of another age. Good people appear the creations of a good time that is past, but they are forever loved. If by chance, some be still left, they are no longer in style and no longer imitated. Oh, the misery of this our age, which holds virtue alien and evil the order of the day! Let the man of conscience live as he can, not as he might wish. Let him hold as better what fortune has conceded him than what she has denied him.

121

Do not make a production of the trivial. Just as some can make a tale out of anything, so others can make a business of everything. They always speak importantly. They take all things seriously, making of everything either a case or a mystery. To convert petty annoyances into matters of importance is to become seriously involved in nothing. It is to miss the point, to carry on the chest what has been cast from the shoulders. Many things which were something, by being left alone became nothing; others which were nothing, became much because messed into. In its beginnings it is easy to make an end of anything, but not so, later. For many a time the remedy itself brings out the disease. By no means the worst rule of life, to let things rest.

122

Distinction in speech and in action: It makes a large place for itself everywhere and compels respect in advance. It shows itself in everything: in bearing, in talk, at times in the walk, or even in the look, and in the desire. A great triumph thus to win all hearts. For it is not the fruit of a silly forwardness or of a stupid superciliousness, but of a becoming authority born of a superior mind and helped along by merit.

123

A person without affectation: The greater your qualifications, the less the need to affect any of them, for this vulgarly insults all the rest. Affectation is as distasteful to everybody else as it is painful to the one who practices it, who lives a martyr to apprehension, and is tormented by punctiliousness. The greatest virtues lose their merit when they are thought to be children of violence rather than innocence, since all that is natural is always more pleasing than the artificial. The affected will always be held foreign to the one who affects it. The better a thing is done, the less need it has to betray effort, because the perfect must appear as fallen ready-made from heaven. Nor, in order to escape affectation, become affected in trying not to be. The person of discrimination never exhibits his virtues, for it is through their very concealment that they awaken the interest of others. Twice great is the one who carries all his perfections within himself, and none in his own conceit. By indirection, he reaches the goal of plausibility.

124

Strive to be in demand. Few attain to such grace in the eyes of others, and if the others are persons of understanding, joy indeed! It is typical to be·indifferent toward those who are finished. But there are ways of gaining this prize of continued adoration: Excellence in a post, and excellence of talent, assure it. Charm of manner is also efficacious. For eminence is built upon such properties, because of which it is soon discovered that the person needed the office less than the office needed the person. The posts bring honor to some, and others bring honor to their posts. But there is no glory in being held good because the one who succeeded you is bad. This does not prove that you are wanted back, but only that the other is wanted out.

125

No enemy list: It is a fault in yourself to point to the shame of another. Some seek with the spots of others to cover their own: either to white-wash them, or thus to console themselves, which is the solace of fools. The breath smells badly from those who are the sewers of a city's filth, in which stuff the one who digs deepest is most soiled. Few are free from some original sin, be it of commission or omission. Only the sins of little-known people are little-known. Let the alert person guard against being a recorder of evil, for it is to be a person despised, and one who even though human, is inhuman.

126

One is not a fool who commits foolishness, but the one who having done so does not know how to conceal it. If your merits should be kept under seal, how much more your demerits. All people go wrong, but with this difference: The intelligent cover up what they have committed, and the fools expose even what they may commit. A good name rests more upon what is concealed than upon what is revealed, for one who cannot be good must be cautious. The sins of great persons should be regarded as mere eclipses of the heavenly bodies. Let it be a mistake to confide your errors even to a friend, for were it possible, you should not disclose them to yourself. But since this is impossible, make use here of that other principle of life which is: Learn how to forget.

127

Self-confidence in everything: It is the life of the talents, the flower of speech, the soul of action, the halo of splendor itself. Every other grace is merely the apparel of nature, but self-confidence is the orna-ment of grace itself, showing even in the daily round. For the most part it is a bequest of fortune, owing little to schooling, to which it is superior. Being more than ease, and approaching daring, it takes unem-barrassment for granted and adds perfection to performance. Without it all beauty is dead, and all grace graceless. For it transcends courage, wisdom, prudence, majesty itself. It is the courteous way about in every business, and the polite way out of every embarrassment.

128

Of lofty ambition: It is the first requisite to make the hero. It spurs one to every species of greater attainment: improving taste, quickening the heart, stimulating the mind, ennobling the spirit, and dignifying majesty. Whatever it settles upon it glorifies. Even when at times the bitterness of fate brings defeat, it returns anew to the conflict, strengthened in will even as it was frustrated in accomplishment. Magnanimity, generosity, and every heroic virtue recognize in it their source.

129

Never complain. To complain constantly only discredits you. Better to be an example of boldness against passion than of timidity under compassion. To complain is to open the way to the listener to the very thing of which you complain. By giving notice of a first insult, you make excuse for a second. Many a person with a complaint of injustices past has invited more. By crying for help or for pity, he has merely gained sufferance or even contempt. Better politics to laud the generosity of one and thus to lay obligations upon another. To recite the favors done by those absent is to compel them from those present. For this is to sell the esteem in which you are held by the one to the other. So a person of sense will never publish abroad either the slights or the wrongs he may have suffered, but only the honor in which he is held. This will serve better to constrain his friends and to restrain his enemies.

130

Act, and give the appearance of acting. Things do not pass for what they are, but for what they seem. To have worth, and to know how to show it, is to be worth double. That which is not made apparent is as though it were not, for even justice is not venerated unless it carry the face of justice. Those who are fooled outnumber those who are not, for it is sham that rules. Things are judged by what they look like, even though most things are far different from what they appear. A good exterior is the best recommendation of the excellence of the interior.

131

Gallantry of condition: The soul has its courage, a gallantry of the spirit which lifts up the heart. But it is not found in all people, because it calls for magnanimity. Its first affair is to speak well of an enemy and to deal with him even better. It shines most brightly in moments most opportune for revenge, when, instead of ignoring them, it brings them into higher relief by converting victory into an unexpected generosity. Even so it remains politic, the flower of diplomacy: never displaying triumph because it displays nothing, and although merit attained it, modestly concealing the fact.

132

Know the value of reconsideration. To appeal for review makes for safety, and especially where dissatisfaction is evident, gains time, either to soften judgment or to strengthen it. New reasons appear to support and to confirm the decision. If something is to be granted, then the gift well-considered is cherished more than that bestowed in the rush of the moment. For what has been longed for is always prized more highly. And if something must be refused, time gives opportunity for discovering how best and most softly to say no, that it be better flavored. Usually when the first heat of desire has passed off, the disappointment of refusal appears less cold-blooded. To one who pleads too urgently, concession should always be made tardily, for that trick denies attention.

133

Better a fool with the crowd, than a sage by yourself. The politicians say that if all people are fools, no one of them can be counted such; wherefore the wise person who stands apart must be a fool. It is important, therefore, to go with the flow. The greatest knowledge at times is to know nothing, or to affect to know nothing. We have to live with others, and the stupid make up the majority. To live alone one must have within oneself either much of God, or much of the beast: I am strongly urged to turn this aphorism about and say: Better wise with the rest of the wise, than a fool by yourself. Still some find distinction in making fools of themselves.

134

Double the necessities of life: It is to double life. For you may not depend solely upon, or be limited to, any one thing, however extraordinary it may be. Everything should be had twice over, and especially the means of life, goodwill, and satisfaction. The face of the moon changes constantly even though it rests upon the permanent. How much more do the things of this life, which depend upon a human charity that is most fragile. Lay up a reserve against this brittleness. Let it be the policy of your life to have in double store the means for living well and comfortably. Just as nature has given us doubly of those members which are most important and most exposed, so let art assure us doubly of those things upon which life itself depends.

135

Do not carry a spirit of contradiction, for it is to be freighted with stupidity and with peevishness. Your intelligence should plot against it. Though it may well be the mark of mental genius to see objection, a wrangler about everything cannot escape being marked the fool. He makes guerrilla warfare of quiet conversation, and so becomes more of an enemy to his intimates than to those with whom he will have nothing to do. It is in the most savory morsel that the spine which gets caught hurts most, and so it is with contradiction in moments of happy converse. Such a person is an offensive fool, who adds the beastly to the untamed within himself.

136

Put yourself in the middle of things, to get at once at the heart of the business. Most roam around in useless millings, either about the edge or in the scrub of a tiresome verbosity. Without striking upon the substance of the matter, they make a hundred turns about a point, wearying themselves and wearying others. Yet they never arrive at the center of what is important. It is the product of a scattered brain that does not know how to get itself together. They spend time and exhaust patience over that which they should leave alone, and afterwards are short of both for what they did leave alone.

137

Let the wise person be self-sufficient. One who was all in all to himself, when carrying himself hence, carried everything with him. If one learned friend can rebuild for you Rome and all the rest of the world, be such a friend to yourself, and you will be able to live alone. For to whom might you be beholden, when there exists no better mind and no better judgment than your own? Learn to rely upon yourself, because it makes for that happy supremacy which is like the supremacy of the Highest. One who is thus able to live within himself is like the brute in nothing, like the sage in much, and like God in everything.

138

The sense to let things settle: Especially when the public or the private sea is most turbulent. There come whirlwinds into human traffic, storms of passion, when it is wise to seek a safe harbor with smoother waters. Many times an evil is made worse by the remedies used. Here leave things to nature, or there to God. The learned physician needs just as much wisdom in order not to prescribe, as to prescribe. Often the greater art lies in doing nothing. The way to quiet the turbulence of a mob is to withdraw your hand and let it quiet itself. To concede today may be the best way to succeed tomorrow. It takes little to muddy a spring, nor does it clear by being stirred, but by being left alone. There is no better remedy for turmoil than to let it take its course, for so it comes to rest of itself.

139

Know your unlucky days. For such there are, when nothing goes right, and even if the game changes, the bad luck does not. You know them after two throws of the dice, and you retire or play on, depending upon whether this is such a day or not. Even the mind has its periods, for no one is wise at all hours. It takes luck to think straight, just as it takes luck to write a good letter. For all good things have their season: beauty not always being in style, judgment itself turning traitor, now making us too soft, now too harsh. Thus anything to come off well must be of its day. Just so does everything go wrong with some, and everything go right with others, and with less effort. All they touch stands ready, the spirit is well-disposed, the mind is alert, and their star is in the ascendant. Then is the hour to strike and not to squander the least advantage. But the person of judgment will not let just one throw augur the day unlucky or lucky. For the former may have been only mischance, and the latter only happy accident.

140

Hit at once upon the good in everything. It is the reward of good taste: The bee goes directly to the sweet for its comb, and the adder to the bitter for its venom. And so with the tastes of people, some to the good, some to the bad. There is nothing that does not hold some good. Especially if it be a book, because of the thought it may contain. But the minds of some people are of such unhappy frame that out of a thousand good points they strike upon the lone bad. This they trot out and carp upon, mere scavengers of the soil of other people's purposes and minds, and mere compilers of the sins of others. Better punishment for their bad choice, than occupation for their cleverness. They lead a sad life, for they batten forever on the bitter, and make bread of refuse. Happier the taste of those who among a thousand evils strike at once upon the single good, even though present only by chance.

141

Not infatuated with your own voice: Small comfort to be satisfied with yourself, if you do not satisfy others. General disdain usually punishes such conceit. One who would pay by personal note owes everybody, for to wish to be the speaker and the auditor too does not go well. If to talk to yourself is nonsense, to wish to listen to yourself, and this before others, is nonsense twice over. It is the habit of these people to speak to some such refrain as, I am about to say, or, Ahem. All torture to those who must listen. Every moment they strain the ear for approbation or flattery, to drive people crazy. The inflated always mouth other people's words, and as their talk parades in the buskins of arrogance, their every word calls forth the stupid approval of some fool: Well said!

142

Never hold to the wrong side out of stubbornness, just because your adversary anticipated you and chose the right. For then you are beaten from the start and will have to retire in disgrace. The right is never saved through the wrong. The opponent was clever to preempt the better side and you stupid to oppose him by taking up the worse. Stubbornness in action is more ensnarling than stubbornness in speech, for there is greater risk in doing than in talking. The vulgarity of these clowns is that they do not observe the truth, because they lie; nor their own interest, because they are on the wrong side. A heedful person stands always on the side of reason and never that of passion, either because he foresaw it from the first, or found it better afterwards. For if the adversary is a fool he may on his own account change face, adopt the opposite side and so weaken his position. But the only way to drive him from the better side is to seize it yourself, for his stupidity will make him drop it, and his obstinacy free you from your own.

143

Not a smart aleck, in order to escape being commonplace: Either extreme discredits you. Every act that deviates from the serious borders upon the foolish. A paradox in essence is a species of pious fraud, which is admired because of its freshness and its piquancy. But later when its trickiness is discovered, it fares so badly that it is scorned. It is a kind of imposition, and in political matters, the ruin of the state. Those who cannot or dare not do something really great over the road of merit repair to the paradoxical, to be admired of fools, and to become a red light to the prudent. It is the mark of a disordered judgment, and on this account should be forsworn by the discerning. Though at times it may not be founded upon error, it is rarely founded upon truth, to the great hazard of all that is important.

144

Enter into the plans of another in order to come out with your own. It is the strategic means to an end; even in heavenly matters, Christian fathers inculcate this holy principle. It is a great trick because it baits useful enterprise by gaining goodwill. For while it looks as though his ends were being served, the maneuver serves no less to open the way to your own. But the business may not be entered upon by the bungler, especially where the ground is dangerous. With persons whose first response inclines to be no, it is well to cover the play. Thus the difficulty of concession may not be observed, especially if it look like a reversal in judgment. This bit of advice belongs to those rules that have to do with action through indirection, all of which are exquisitely subtle.

145

Do not exhibit your sore finger for all to strike upon. And do not complain of it, for malice always pounds where it hurts most. No use to get angry, for this will only add to the general amusement. Evil intent goes sneaking around to uncover the infirmity. It prods about in a thousand different ways to discover where the suffering is greatest, until it hits the spot. The circumspect never reveal feelings or disclose a disease, be it acquired or inherited, for fate herself is pleased at times to scourge us, and just where it hurts most. She always mortifies us in the flesh. On which account never disclose either what worries or what refreshes, the one that it may pass, the other that it may last.

146

Look beneath: For ordinarily things are far other than they seem. The dullness which does not seek to pass beyond the rind is due to be increasingly disillusioned if it gets deeper into the interior. The false is forever the lead in everything, continually dragging along the fools. The truth brings up the rear, is late, and limps along upon the arm of time. The person of insight will save for it at least the half of that faculty which our great mother has wisely given us twice. Deceit is superficial, wherefore the superficial are taken in at once. The person of substance lives safely within himself, to be better treasured of his colleagues and of those who know.

147

Open to suggestion: None is so perfect as to not at times need a monitor, for he is incurably the fool who will not listen. Even the most high should lend ear to friendly advice, for sovereignty itself may not shut off wise counsel. There are people who cannot be saved because they cannot be reached. They hurl themselves to destruction because none dares to approach to restrain them. The most faultless should leave open one door to friendship, for it may prove a portal of succor. Place should be made for one friend at least to advise without embarrassment, and even to find fault. But this privilege should rest upon his rightness, and upon our trust in him and his understanding. But we need not bare our inner selves to just anybody, not even our reputation. Keep within the closet of your soul the faithful mirror of a trusted friend to whom you may turn, and from whom you will take correction when in error.

148

Have the art of conversation, for it is the hallmark of the person. No human enterprise demands greater heed for so large a part of everyday life, whence its dangers or its advantages. If care is necessary to write a letter, which is conversation studied and committed to paper, how much more is necessary in everyday speech, when the intelligence must at every moment pass examination? Skilled people take the pulse of the soul at the tongue, in which knowledge the Sage of sages said: Speak, if you would that I know you. Some hold that the art of conversation lies in its artlessness, that it should lack formality, like the clothing. This may hold between friends. But where it is to gain respect, it must have more form, to display better the substance of the person. To strike it right you must be able to adapt yourself to the mind and to the spirit of your company. Do not make yourself a carping critic of words, or you will be held the grammatical fool; nor yet the opponent of what is reasonable, or all will flee you and look doubtfully upon what you have to say. Discretion in what is said is better far than eloquence.

149

Know how to let the blame slip upon another. To carry a shield against malevolence is the wise strategy of those who govern. A thing not born of weakness, as the envious think, but of greater strength is to have on hand someone to shoulder the blame for failure, or to take on the punishment of general abuse. Not everything can come off well, nor everybody be satisfied. Wherefore provide yourself with someone to atone for your errors and be a well for tears, even though it cost you some of your pride.

150

Know how to sell your wares. Their intrinsic worth is not enough, for all do not turn the goods nor look deep. Most run where the crowd is, running because the others run. It is a great art to know how to sell: at times by praising the goods, because praise excites desire; at times by giving them a good name, which is a great way to exalt them; but always cloaking any show of affectation in the matter. To say that they are intended only for the sophisticated is to whet the public appetite. For everybody thinks himself sophisticated, and if he is not, then his sense of lack will spur on his desire. Never should your business be accounted easy or ordinary, for to make a thing easy is to make it common. All have an itch for the unusual because it is more desired alike by the taste and by the intelligence.

151

Think ahead: Today for tomorrow, and for many days beyond. The wisest of precautions is to take time for this, for to the ready there are no accidents, and to the forewarned no dangers. Do not wait to think until you are overcome, but be forehanded. Anticipate with matured reflection the worst outrages of destiny. The pillow is a silent Sibyl, and to sleep upon an enterprise avails more than to be sleepless under it. Some act first and think afterwards, which means they must concern themselves more with the excuses for their acts than with the consequences. Others think neither before nor after, when all life should be continuous thinking in order to hit upon the right way. It is reflection and foresight that assure freedom to life.

152

Never accompany one who puts you in the shade, either because more virtuous or more vicious. The one of greater capacity gains the greater recognition, and so will always play the main role and you the second.

If any glory devolves upon you, it will be through the other's merits. The moon shines only when alone among the stars; for as the sun rises, it either fades or goes out. Never approach one who eclipses you, but only one who increases your luster. It was by such means that the wise Fabula could look beautiful at the feast of Mars, and shine against the homeliness and the slovenliness of her maids. Neither endanger yourself by taking on the wrong side nor grant honor to another at the cost of your own reputation. To be made, walk with your superiors, but if made, with the mediocre.

153

Beware of entering to fill a great gap. But if you do commit yourself, let it be in the knowledge that you overfill it. It will be necessary to be worth double merely to seem to equal your predecessor. Just as it is wise to see to it that one who succeeds you is such that you are wished back, it is similarly wise to observe that the one who preceded you does not eclipse you. A hard task to fill a great hiatus, for what has gone before always appears the better. To balance it does not suffice, because it holds the prior claim. It is therefore necessary to have command of additional gifts in order to dispossess the other of the higher opinion in which she or he is held.

154

Slow to believe, and slow to cherish: Maturity is recognized in the deliberateness with which a person adopts a creed. The false is the ordinary of the day, wherefore let belief be the extraordinary. One who is too quickly convinced must too slowly become unconvinced. But do not exhibit your doubt in the faith of another, for that passes as discourtesy or even insult. Such action holds your witness a cheat, or one cheated. Even this however is not the greatest trouble, but that the unbeliever is marked the liar, since lying is burdened with two evils: It neither believes nor is it believed. Suspension of judgment is always the part of wisdom in a listener, and the remission of faith to authority the part of wisdom in a speaker. Too ready allegiance is a kind of imprudence, for people lie in word as they lie in deed, and the latter is more deadly because more active.

155

Art in rising to anger: Whenever possible, let cold deliberation take the place of sudden outburst. This should not prove difficult for one who has prudence. The first step in rising to anger is to note that you are angry, for that is to enter master of the situation. Having determined the need of it, and its height, and going no further, with this considered judgment let your wrath wax and wane. Know well how to stop and when, for the most difficult feat in racing lies in stopping. It is fine proof of judgment to keep your head when the fools have lost theirs. Every flare of temper is a step downwards from the rational, but properly checked it will not go beyond reason or trample upon conscience. To be master of an angry mood, it is necessary always to ride with the tight rein of attention. Thus you will be the first to mount, if not the last.

156

Friends by choice: For they can be such only after they have been examined with discernment and tested by time: the elect not only of desire, but of judgment. Though this be the most important deed in life, least care is exercised in its prosecution. Intrusion brings some, but chance the most. Since one is known by the friends he keeps, he who is wise never consorts with fools. To find pleasure in a person does not prove him a friend, for this may spring more from the high value set upon his company than upon the confidence felt in his capacity. There are friendships which are legitimate and others which are adulterous: the latter for your delight, the former to fructify your accomplishments. Few are the friends of your self; the most, the friends of your success. The understanding of one good friend avails you more than the good wishes of many others. Wherefore let him be the product of choice and not of accident. One wise friend knows how to relieve you of your burdens which the fool knows only how to put upon you. But do not wish him too good fortune if you would not lose him.

157

Do not be deceived in persons, for it is the worst and the easiest of deceptions. Far better to be cheated in the price than in the goods.

Nothing is more important than to look within. Only there is a difference between knowing merchandise and knowing people. It is a great science to understand the minds of men and to discern their humors: just as important to have studied people as to have studied books.

158

Know how to call forth the best in your friends. There is about this its own kind of good sense. Some are good at a distance, and some nearby. One who is never easy in conversation, may be in correspondence, for distance dulls shortcomings intolerable at hand. A friend should not only bring satisfaction, but stimulation and should have the three qualities of the good: unity, goodness, and truth. A friend is all in all. But few make good friends, and one who does not know how to choose them, makes fewer. To know how to keep friends is more than knowing how to make them. Search out those who promise to last. Though at first they appear young, be content that they will grow old. The best variety undoubtedly are the salted, even though their digestion costs you a measure of effort. None lives so alone as one who lives without friends. Friendship doubles the good, and divides the bad. It is the only defense against misfortune, and the very balm of the spirit.

159

Know how to suffer fools. The wise are always grouchy, for one who grows in wisdom, grows in impatience. One who knows much is harder to satisfy. The first precept of life, according to Epictetus: to be able to suffer. And to this may be reduced the half of all wisdom. If every type of folly must be borne, much patience will be required. At times we suffer most from those upon whom we most depend, which is important because it is a school for self-control. Out of suffering comes holy peace, which is the joy of the world. Let one who cannot gain this state of forbearance take refuge within himself, if it be that he can stand even himself.

160

Be careful what you say, as a matter of caution when with rivals, and as a matter of decency when with the rest. There is always time to add a word, but none in which to take one back. Speak, therefore, as if giving testimony, for the fewer the words, the less the litigation. Make of that which is of no importance the training ground for that which is. Reserve has an aspect of divinity about it. One who is too easy of speech quickly falters and falls.

161

Know your pet failings. Even the most perfect person does not escape them, whether wedded to them or cohabiting with them. They inhabit talent, and the greater the talent, the greater the failing—or the more apparent. They are tolerated not because they are unknown but because they are loved. Two evils joined: a passion, and a passion for something poor. They obscure the perfect, as offensive to the beholder as sweet to the owner. Here is opportunity for self-conquest to make your talents shine forth more brightly. Everyone strikes at once upon your short-comings. So when they arrive to praise the great good in you which they admire, they are affronted to the disparagement of all your other gifts.

162

Know how to triumph over the envious and the malevolent. It is not enough to ignore them, though courtesy is a great virtue. Better to meet them with brave face, for there is not enough praise for one who speaks well of one who speaks ill. There is no vengeance more noble than that which through worth and ability becomes the tormentor and the executioner of the envious. Every success tightens the rope about the neck of the malevolent, and the glory of the envied becomes the hell of the envious. This is the greatest of all punishments: to be made unhappy by another's happiness. The envious dies not once, but as often as the envied is reborn by applause, the enduring fame of the one vying with the enduring torture of the other. For the envied is as immortal in glory as the envious in pain. The trumpet of fame, which sounds the one to life eternal, brings execution to the other, sentenced to be choked to death by envy.

163

Never get involved in misfortune out of pity for the unfortunate. What is the bad luck of the one may well be the good luck of the other, for the one could never be lucky if many others were not unlucky. The characteristic of the unfortunate is to win the favor of those who wish forever to make recompense by senseless charity for the blows of unhappy fate. And so one sees at times a person who was, in prosperity, hated by all, pitied by all in adversity: the hatred for the exalted changed to a sympathy for the one cast down. Let the observant take note of how the cards of fortune are shuffled. There are some who never walk except with the unfortunate. They are cheek by jowl today with the unhappy person, from whom they fled yesterday in his happiness. All of which evidences nobility of the soul but not of the intelligence.

164

Stick your finger in the air in order to discover how a matter will be received, especially if you suspect its success or its sanction. Thus do you gain assurance of its happy outcome, or opportunity either to go forward or to turn back. You test out the public temper by this trick, and if observant learn where you stand: a good thing to know in law, in love, and in government.

165

Make a clean fight. The person of intelligence may be driven to fight, but not to fight dirty. Each must act for what he is, and not for what he is expected to be. To remain polite in a contest is to deserve all praise; fight to win, not only through superior strength, but through superior manner. To win basely is not glorious but humiliating. Always be the better in generosity. The knight does not avail himself of forbidden arms, and such are those of a friendship ended and an enmity started, since one may not so convert a confidence into vengeance. All that smells of treason corrupts a good name. Persons of honor are affronted by the least atom of baseness, for the noble must be kept far from the vile. Glory in the fact that if gallantry, generosity, and fidelity were to perish off this earth, they would still be discoverable in your breast.

166

Distinguish the person of words from the person of deeds. It calls for rare judgment, as does distinction between friends, between persons, or between titles. For the difference is great: To be without good words or evil deeds is little, but to be without bad words or good deeds is less. We cannot feed on words, for they are the wind; nor can we live on mere manner, for that is polite sham. To hunt birds with a light is truly to blind them. Let the pompous inflate themselves on bombast, but words should be the pledge of deeds, for herein lies their value. The trees that bear no fruit, but only leaves, are apt to lack heart. Well to know them, to use the one for its timber, the other for its shade.

167

Know how to help yourself. There is no better companion in the great struggles of life than a stout heart. When it flags it must be supported by the organs that stand about. Anxieties grow less in one who knows how to defend himself. Never surrender to fate, for then she ends by making herself intolerable. Some help themselves little with their burdens; in fact they double them because they do not know how to carry them. One who really knows himself brings thought to the support of his frailties. Wherefore the person of intelligence comes out victorious from under everything, even the unlucky stars.

168

Do not fall into the class of the colossal asses. Such are all the pompous, the presumptuous, the stubborn, the capricious, the too easily led, the freaks, the affected, the facetious, the faddists, the perverse, the sectarians of all kinds, and the whole generation of the intemperate. Monsters, all of them, of impertinence. Every distortion of the spirit is more deforming than one of the body, because it degrades a superior beauty. But who can bring order out of such general confusion? Where the captain of the soul is missing, no use to look for direction. What was meant as the gentle hint of derision is falsely imagined to be applause.

169

A miss counts more than a hundred hits. None looks upon the sun in its splendor, but all in its eclipse. Vulgar history takes no count of what went right, only of what went wrong. Better known is all evil through gossip than all good through acclaim. Many were never noticed until they failed. Neither do all the accomplishments of a person taken together avail to blot out a single small failure. Let every person be clear in this matter: that cognizance will be taken by the tongue of slander of everything done badly, but of nothing done well.

170

In all matters keep something in reserve. It is to insure your position. Not all your wit must be spent nor all your energies sapped every time. Even of what you know keep a rear guard, for it is to double your advantage always to have in reserve something to call upon when danger threatens. The support may mean more than the attack, because it exhibits faith and fortitude. An intelligent person always plays safe, wherefore even here that sharp paradox holds: More is the half than the whole.

171

Do not squander favor. Great friends are for great occasions; so do not waste a great generosity upon a trivial matter, for that is to squander goodwill. Let the holy anchor always be kept against the worst storm. If the great is spent upon the small, what will be left for afterwards? There is nothing more protective than a protector, nor anything more precious today than goodwill. It makes or unmakes the world, even to giving it life, or killing it. Persons of wisdom, even as they are favored by nature and by fame, are despised by fortune; so it marks their better judgment to have and to hold friends rather than slaves.

172

Do not engage with one who has nothing to lose. It is to fight at a disadvantage, for the other enters without encumbrance, because unaccoutred even of shame. Having auctioned off everything, he has nothing more to lose, and so may allow himself every insolence. Never expose to such great hazard your treasured reputation. What cost you years to attain can go to perdition, and there be lost in one unlucky moment what has cost much precious sweat. It makes the person of honor pause and consider what is at stake. While regarding his own good name, he looks at that of the other, and so becomes entangled only after great consideration. He proceeds with such caution that prudence is given time to recall and put in safekeeping a reputation. Not even victory can bring in as much as was risked when a good name was merely exposed to loss.

173

Don't be fragile in your dealings, least of all with your friends. Some crack with the greatest ease, showing that they are made of poor stuff. They fill themselves with imagined wrongs, and all others with vexation. They show their natures to be more soft than the eyes themselves, so none may touch them, either in fun or in earnest. Such trifles bruise that real hurt is not necessary. They must watch their step who have dealings with them, alert always to their great sensitiveness, and on guard against every draft, since the slightest disturbance upsets them. Worshipers of their imagined honor, these people are commonly selfish, the slaves of their whims, for which they would sacrifice everything. But the heart of friendship is like the heart of a diamond in its enduringness and in its firmness.

174

Don't live in haste. To know how to spread things out is to know how to enjoy them. Many have finished with their luck before they have finished with their lives; they miss happiness because they do not know how to enjoy. And so they would afterwards turn back, for they have so quickly outrun themselves. Stage drivers of life, to the general runaway they add their own impatient whip. They seek to swallow in a day what can scarce be digested in a lifetime. They live swiftly through every joy, eating up the years to come. And as they crowd forward in such haste, they are quickly through with everything. Even in the quest after knowledge it is well to have reserve, in order not to learn those things which are better not learned. The days of life outnumber the joys; so go slowly in enjoyment, but in work make haste. For the day's labors are gladly finished, but not so gladly its joys.

175

A person of substance: One who is has little fondness for those who are not. Eminence that does not rest upon a sure foundation is unfortunate. Not all who seem to be are fully human, but fakes, conceived as hybrids and born humbugs. Many more are like them, in that they build them up. They take more delight in the false, which promises most because most, than in the truth, which promises little, because so little. In the end their shams fare badly, for they lack foundation in truth. Only truth can bestow a true reputation, and only solid character prove profitable. One fraud makes necessary another and another; and so the whole of what is built up is flimsy. Resting upon air, it is destined to return to earth. Never has mere scenery lasted, for an outward show that promises too much is sufficient to make itself suspect, just as that which is overly proved is held impossible.

176

Know, or listen to one who knows. You cannot live without knowledge, either your own or borrowed. But there are many who do not know that they know nothing, and others who think that they know, but know nothing. These deformities of the mind are incurable, whence it is that the ignorant neither know themselves nor yet how to gain what they lack. Some would be wise if they did not believe themselves wise. Wherefore it comes to pass that the oracles of wisdom, even though few, live neglected because no one consults them. It does not dwarf grandeur or argue against capacity to seek advice. Surely to seek advice brings credit: Better to reason it out than to fight it out with misfortune.

177

Avoid familiarities in social relations. Neither practice them yourself nor permit them to be practiced upon you. One who allows them, surrenders the superiority his character merits, and respect to boot. The stars do not get intimate with us, but hold themselves aloof in their splendor. For the divine demands respect, and everything too human makes easy disrespect. Earthly affairs even as they become more human, become more cheap, because through communion they communicate their tawdriness, which distance concealed. It is well never to get on common ground with anyone: not with your betters, because that is dangerous, and not with your inferiors, because that is indecent.

And least of all with the common herd. For it is insolent because it is ignorant, and failing to recognize the favor, presumes upon it as a right. Intimacy borders on vulgarity.

178

Trust your heart, especially when it is being proved. For it is never untrue to itself. Often foretelling what is of greatest import, it is a veritable inward oracle. Many have died of what they feared; but why did they fear without doing something about it? Some have a heart most faithful, the advantage of a great nature, which always forewarns them and sounds the alarm in order that danger may be met. There is no sense in sallying forth looking for trouble; but if such sally be made, let it be to engage and defeat the enemy.

179

Reserve is the seal of capacity. The heart with no secrets is an open letter. Secrets are buried best where there is depth, for there lie caverns and bays where treasure may be hid. Profundity is the product of a great mastery over self, and to be master in this is to be a conqueror indeed. The heart must pay tribute to all to whom it reveals itself. In inner quiet lies the salvation of the spirit. What threatens reserve are the attacks of others: those of contradiction, in order to excite it; or those of baiting, in order to drive it from cover. Such will only make the observant shut up more tightly. Those things which are to be done should not be talked about, and those which have been talked about should not be done.

180

Never be misled by what your foe does. If he is a fool he will not do what a wiser thinks best, because he never knows what is best. And if he is a person of discretion, not then, because he wishes to cloak his intent, even to the point of forestalling the other. Every situation must be looked at from two points of view and be considered first from one side and then the other, to be disposed of from either angle. Human minds differ greatly. So let judgment remain alert, not so much because of what is happening, as because of what may.

181

Without lying, do not speak the whole truth. There is nothing that requires more careful handling than the truth, for it is a bleeding from the heart. It is just as necessary to know how to utter the truth as to know how to hush it. A whole reputation for uprightness may be ruined with a single lie, for a lie is held treachery, and the liar a traitor, which is worse. Not all truths may be spoken, because some matter to us, and some matter to others.

182

A bit of audacity in everything is common sense. It is to step down your concept of the others in order not to believe them so exalted that you fear them. Never allow your imagination to surrender to your heart. Some appear great until you meet them, but communion with them serves more to bring disillusion to you than exaltation to them. None gets beyond the confines of the human; there is in everyone a "but": in some, of the heart, and in some, of the spirit. Rank bestows apparent superiority, but only rarely is it accompanied by personal qualification. For fate has a way of avenging greatness of office by meanness of the occupant. The imagination always hurries forward and paints things brighter than they are: conceding not only what is, but what might be. Because experience so often disillusions, let calm judgment correct the picture, in order that stupidity be not too bold, nor virtue too timorous. If self-confidence has at times availed the simpleton, how much more valuable to the wise!

183

Hold to nothing too violently: Every fool stands convinced, and everyone convinced is a fool. The faultier a person's judgment, the firmer his conviction. Even with the proof on your side, it is well to make concession, for your reasons are known and your gallantry is recognized. More is lost in contention than can be gained in consummation, for such does not defend the truth, but only exhibits bad manner. Blockheads are difficult or impossible of conversion, for when conviction is joined to obstinacy, both are indissolubly married to stupidity. Inflexibility should lie in the will and not in the judgment. Yet there are exceptions when you may not yield without danger of being twice conquered: first in your decision, and then in its execution.

184

Do not stand on ceremony. For even in a king this affectation was celebrated as something ridiculous. Punctiliousness frets the spirit, and yet whole nations put on such show. The apparel of fools is patched of such pieces. Idolaters of their self-importance they prove it to be founded upon little, because constantly in fear that something will injure it. Well to demand respect, but not so well to be considered a grand master of pomposity. Yet it is the truth that the person without all show must need be possessed of the greatest virtues. Good form should not be affected, nor yet despised. But it does not evidence greatness to be a mere stickler about trifles.

185

Never risk your reputation on a single shot, for if you miss, the loss is irreparable. It is very easy to go wrong once, and especially the first time. Not always is this the right moment, wherefore it is said: Wait for your day. Assure yourself therefore of a second chance through the first, if it went wrong or if it went right. Let the first have been the pawn for the second. Always hold in reserve recourse to something better, and the reputation of having something more. Everything depends so very much upon circumstance that the happiness of a happy ending is rare.

186

Know evil, no matter how much it is sanctioned. Let the person of intelligence not fail to recognize it. Even if clothed in brocade or crowned with gold, it cannot hide its bane. Slavery does not lose its infamy, however noble the master. The vices may stand high, but they are not high. Some see a great person afflicted with this vice or that, but they do not see that he is great not because of it but in spite of it. The portrait of the person high up is so convincing that even his deformities persuade. Wherefore flattery at times mimics them, not seeing that if in the great such things are overlooked, in the small they are looked down upon.

187

All that gains approval, do yourself, and all that gains disapproval, do through another. By the first you invite affection, and by the second you avoid hatred. More satisfying to the great to do good than to receive it, for it is the joy of the spirit. Rarely can one give pain to another without suffering it himself, either through compassion or through commiseration. Even God does not work without reward or without retribution, dealing out the good directly and the bad indirectly. Wherefore keep at hand someone to absorb the recoils of discontent, which are hatred and abuse. Madness in a crowd is like madness in dogs, who failing to recognize the cause of their suffering, turn upon their muzzles which though not at fault, are made to suffer as though they were.

188

Be the bearer of good news. It proves your good taste. It shows that you knew the best elsewhere, and that you may be relied upon for correct opinion on what is here. One who knew quality yesterday will know it again today. To commend what is praiseworthy is to make for conversation and for emulation. It is the polite way of paying obeisance to the perfect in those about you. Others, on the contrary, always choose to be the bearers of evil report, flattering those present by detraction of those absent. They come off well with the superficial, who do not recognize this trick of speaking evil of the one to the other. Some have made politics of the matter of cherishing more the mediocrities of today than the great of yesterday. Let the astute see through these cunnings of the bearer, and be not dismayed by the tall tales of the one, or inflated by the flattery of the other. Realize that behavior with the one group is as with the other, changing in mind and in action according to the spot at which the tale bearer has arrived.

189

Know how to make use of another's want; for if it rises to the level of lust, it becomes the most effective of thumbscrews. The philosophers declare desire to be nothing; the politicians, everything. The latter are the wiser. They make of the desires of others the stepping-stones to their own ends. They utilize the opportunity, and by emphasizing the difficulties of satisfying such desires, sharpen the appetite. For they are assured of more through the heat of passion, than through the luke-warmness of possession. As resistance to what is wanted increases, desire grows. A very subtle way of accomplishing your own purposes, to keep people dependent upon you.

190

Find consolation in everything. Even the worthless live forever. There is no sorrow unmitigated. The fools find consolation in their luck, which makes proverbial the luck of the hunchback. To live long, it is only necessary to be worth little. It is the cracked pot that is never broken, for which reason it irritates because it lasts so long. It is against those who really count that fortune holds her grudge, for she bestows length of days upon the bums and shortness of days upon those who are something. The greater their worth, the sooner they die; while those of no profit live forever, at times because they seem to, at others because they really do. To one in misery it looks as though fortune and death had both conspired to forget him.

191

Do not consider an account squared by mere excess of manner, for it is a species of fraud. In order to bewitch, some people don't need the herbs of Thessaly, for they enchant fools with one airy wave of the hat which makes them swoon. They make toadying a business, and pay their way with the wind of fine words. One who promises everything, promises nothing. And yet one who merely promises ensnares the fools. Real manner is an obligation, but its affectation is a deception, especially if out of order. It is not decency then, but subserviency. All of which exhibits respect not for the person but for the person's goods, and pays compliment not to his talents which are apparent but to his profits which are hoped for.

192

A person of peace, a person of years: In order to live, let live. The peaceful not only live, but they reign. Lend your ears and your eyes, but hold your tongue. The day without strife makes the night with its sleep. To live long and to live in joy is to live twice, and the fruit of peace. One has everything who gives no concern to what does not concern him. Nothing more purposeless than to see purpose in everything, for it is equally stupid to break the heart over what is not your business and not to set your teeth into that which is.

193

Look to the one who comes in as agent for another's concern in order to go out with his own. There is no defense against trickery like that of watchfulness: against a code, a good decoder. Some make of the affairs of others their own. Unless their purpose is recognized, your every move will only get you deeper into the job of withdrawing from the fire the chestnuts of another, to the great damage of your own hand.

194

Have a sane assessment of yourself and your aims, particularly when they first come to life. All have a high opinion of themselves, particularly those with least reason. Each dreams himself a fortune, and imagines himself a prodigy. Hope wildly promises everything, and time then fulfills nothing. These things torment the spirit, as the imagined gives way before the truth. Wherefore let the person of judgment correct his blunders, and even though hoping for the best, always expect the worst, in order to be able to accept with equanimity whatever comes. It is well, of course, to aim somewhat high in order to near the mark, but not so high that you miss altogether a starting upon your life's job. To make this proper estimate of yourself is absolutely necessary, for without experience it is very easy to confuse the conjectured with the fact. There is no greater panacea against all that is foolish, than understanding. Wherefore let every person know what is the sphere of his abilities, and his place, and thus be able to make the picture of himself coincide with the actual.

195

Know how to appraise. There is none who cannot be the master of another in something, or having excelled, cannot be excelled. To know how to pick the fruit from every person's tree is profitable knowledge. The wise person knows the value of everything because he recognizes the good in everything, and knows how much it takes to

make things good. Only a fool is scornful of everything, through ignorance of what is good, and through bad choice of what is no good.

196

Know your star. None is so forgotten as to have none, and if yours be
an unlucky one, it is because you do not know your own. Some stand
high in the favor of princes and of potentates, knowing not why or
wherefore, but that their luck followed them. To help it along they
needed only industry. Others discover themselves in the graces of the
wise. Some are better received of one nation than another, or made
more welcome in this city than in that. Thus also is more satisfaction
to be gained in one position or place than in another, even though in
what they offer they appear to be alike or actually are identical. Fate
shuffles the cards as and when she chooses. Let each know her own
star as she knows her own mind, for it determines whether she shall
perish or be saved. Let her know how to follow it and keep pace with
it, never mistaking it. For that would be to miss the polar star itself, to
which the nearby Little Bear is constantly pointing.

197

Do not saddle yourself with fools. He who does not know them is one,
and he who, knowing them, does not shake them off is a bigger one. For
they are dangerous in the daily round, and deadly as confidants. Even
if at times their cowardice or the watchful eye of another restrains them,
in the end they commit some foolishness or speak it, which if they
tarry over it is only to make it worse. Slight aid to another's reputation,
one who has none himself. They are full of woes, the welts of their
follies, and they trade in the one for the other. But this about them is
not so bad: that even though the wise are of no service to them, they
are of much service to the wise, either as example or as warning.

198

Be known as transplantable. There are exotics which in order to
flower need change of soil, and especially those most rare. The home
country is a stepmother to its own great talent; jealousy rules her as
the land itself, and she remembers better the weakness in which a
person started than the strength to which he grew. A needle gains

distinction when passed from one country into another, and glass makes diamonds look cheap when carried elsewhere. All that is foreign is cherished, at times because it comes from afar, at times because it arrives complete and in its perfection. There are people, once the despised of their circle, who today are the honored of the world. They are respected by their compatriots and those foreign; by the one, because they are seen from a distance, and by the other, because they come from a distance. One will never pay homage to the idol upon the altar who knew it as a stump in the forest.

199

Know how to make a place for yourself through desert, and not by pushing. The right road to distinction is that of merit, and when industry is joined to worth, it is a shortcut to the stars. But mere goodness is not enough, and pushing is unbecoming. For then things arrive so soiled that they produce loathing. Best is the middle course between merit and a knowledge of how to usher yourself in.

200

Leave something to be desired, in order not through glut to become unhappy. For the body should want air, and the spirit have its longings. When all is yours, all turns to ashes and disappoints. Even the mind must be left its passion to know, to pique its curiosity and to keep hope alive. A surfeit of happiness is fatal. In bestowing reward it is wisdom never to gratify. When nothing more is to be wished for, everything is to be feared: the most unfortunate of fortunes, for where desire ends, apprehension begins.

201

All are fools who seem to be, and half of those who do not. The world is full of folly and if there be any wisdom in it, this is folly compared to that of heaven. But the greatest fool is the one who does not know himself one, and declares all others such. For to be wise, it is not enough to seem it, least of all to yourself. One knows who knows that he does not know; and one does not see who does not see what others see. With the whole world full of fools, there is none who thinks himself one or even suspects it.

202

Words and deeds make the consummate person. It is to voice what is good and to do what is honorable; the first evidences a good head, the second a good heart. Together they give birth to a great soul. Words are the ghosts of deeds; the former are the ewes, the latter the rams. Of greater moment to be cheered, than to be the cheerleader. To say something is easy, but to do something is difficult. Achievement is the substance of life, and praise, its decoration. Greatness in action endures, greatness in words passes. For deeds are the fruits of the mind which, when wise, make triumphant.

203

Recognize the eminent of your time. They will not be many: one Phoenix in all the world, one great captain, one perfect orator, one sage in the whole of a century, one illustrious king among the many. It is the mediocrities that make up the crowd both in number and in kind. For the great are few, because they require the cloak of perfection. The higher their rating, the greater the difficulty of achieving the top. Many have seized for themselves the surname of great, from Caesar or Alexander, but in vain. For without deeds, the voice is not more than a bit of air. Few Senecas have had their habitation among us, and fame celebrates but one Apelles.

204

Approach the easy as though it were difficult and the difficult as though it were easy. The first, lest overconfidence make you careless, and the second, lest faintheartedness make you afraid. Nothing more is required in order to do nothing than to think it done; to go at the job, on the other hand, accomplishes the impossible. But the greatest undertakings should not be overly pondered, lest contemplation of difficulties too clearly foreseen appall you.

205

Know the value of disdain. It is a trick for the attainment of an end, to be contemptuous of it: The quarry which cannot be captured while pursued, commonly falls into our hands if we only halt. As all things temporal are but the shadows of the heavenly, they become ghostly in this also: that they flee from the pursuer and pursue one who flees from them. Disdain, moreover, is the most politic form of vengeance. A rare maxim of the wise never to defend yourself with the pen, for it leaves a mark that serves more to glorify the adversary than to check his impudence. A trick of the worthless, to appear the adversaries of great persons in order indirectly to make themselves as celebrated, as directly they merit nothing. For many would never have been heard of, had their excellent opponents not paid heed to them. There is no revenge like forgetting, for it is to bury them in the dust of their own nothingness. These brash try to immortalize themselves by setting fire to the wonders of the world and the centuries. The way to silence slander is to ignore it; to fight against it is to prejudice your own case. Even though you win you will still have lost, and satisfaction goes to your adversary. For the slightest cloud can darken, even when it cannot obscure the whole of a great name.

206

Observe that the ordinary lies all about, even in Corinth herself, even in the best of families. And each may discover it within the portals of his own house. But beyond the ordinary there flourishes the vulgar, which is worse. This specialty has all the properties of the familiar, as the fragments of a mirror have those of the unbroken, but more jagged. It talks like a fool and impertinently finds fault. It is the great disciple of ignorance, the godfather of idiocy, and the defender of what is not so. For which reason no heed need be paid to what it says, and less to what it thinks. But it is important to know it, in order to get free of it, whether in a person or an object. For whatever smacks of folly is vulgar, and the vulgar are all fools.

207

Use self-restraint, even more so in the case of chance. There are heats of passion in which the reason slides, and there lies danger of perdition. One second of rage, or one of stupid self-satisfaction, brings more in its wake than many hours of listlessness. They occasion in a moment what requires a lifetime to correct. The craftiness of another may thus try to tempt your soul, to discover where you stand, or what you think. Used like a thumbscrew upon your inner self, it can drive the best of minds mad. Match such wiliness by your self-restraint, particularly in fast repartee. Great control is necessary if passion is not to break the bit, for one who has such a horse has a great head; one goes with caution who knows the danger. Light as a word seems to the one who tosses it off, it may seem heavy to the one who catches it and weighs it.

208

Do not die of the fool's sickness. Usually, the wise perish of mental starvation, and the fools of the glut of too much counsel. To die like a fool is to die of too much thinking. Some die because they have sense, and others live because they have none. Thus both are fools: the latter because they do not die of grief, and the former because they do. A fool is one who dies of too much brain. From which it comes that some die of reason and others live for no reason. But with many dying because fools, few fools die.

209

Keep free of popular inanities. This is especially good sense. They are highly esteemed because so well introduced, and many a person who could not be trapped by some particular stupidity, could not escape the general. One vulgar opinion holds that none is content in his fortune even though the best, and that none is discontented with his mind, even though the worst. Another, that all are covetous and look with unhappiness upon what is their own, and with joy upon what is another's. Again, that they of today glorify only the things of yesterday, and those from here only the things from afar. Or that all that is past is better, and everything that is distant, more valuable. As great a fool one who laughs at everything as one who weeps over everything.

210

Know how to play the truth. She is dangerous, and yet the upright person cannot escape speaking her. Here is where art is required. The skilled physicians of the soul have devised a method of sweetening her,

for when she is about to act upon error, she is the quintessence of bitterness. Avail yourself here of the nimbleness of good form, for the
same truth that wheedles one, cudgels another. Be able to speak of
things present in the terms of things past. With one who can understand, a hint is sufficient; but where nothing is sufficient, go dumb.
Princes may not be cured with bitter remedies, so it becomes an art to
know how to gild the naked truth.

211

In heaven all is gladness. In hell all is sorrow. Upon this earth, since it
lies between, sometimes the one, and sometimes the other. We have
our being between the two extremes, and so it partakes of both. Fortune should vary, not all being felicity, nor all adversity. This world is
a zero, and by itself worth nothing, but joined to heaven worth everything. Indifference to your lot is common sense, and not to be
surprised by it, wisdom. Our life becomes more complicated as we go
along, like a comedy. But toward its end it becomes simpler. Keep in
mind, therefore, the happy ending.

212

Keep the ultimate refinements of your art to yourself. This is the law
of the great masters who must themselves employ best the subtleties of
their art even as they teach them. For only thereby do they remain on
top and so the masters. Art must be put into the teaching of art, lest
its source and its capacity be forgotten. Only thus can you maintain
your reputation and the dependence of others upon you. In the business of pleasing and instructing others, this is good advice: Feed their
wonder, and satisfy their anticipation. To have a reserve in everything
is the great law to life and to conquest, especially in those occupations
most exalted.

213

Know how to debate. It is the craft of exploration intended not to
entangle you but to entangle the other. It is a unique form of torture
to make the feelings flinch. Lukewarmness in believing is a true emetic
of the secrets of the heart, a key to the tightest of locked breasts. It

makes possible a most sensitive probing, both of the mind and of the intent. A cautious questioning of the vagaries uttered by another ferrets out the most hidden secrets, drives them into the mouth to be chewed over until they fall from the tongue, to be caught in the snare of your artifice. Reserve on your part makes the other throw it to the winds, whereby his feelings are exposed, even though by any other method his heart would have been closed. The affectation of doubt is the nimblest lock-pick that curiosity can employ in order to discover whatever it seeks or even what it would learn. A good trick on the part of the pupil to bait his teacher, who thereby excites himself to greater effort in the declaration and the foundation of his beliefs. Whence it comes that well-moderated debate makes for most effective teaching.

214

Don't make two inanities of one. All too often in order to repair one foolish step, four more are taken. Or excuse is made for one dumb trick with a second and a greater. Folly is either of the house of lies, or lies are of the house of folly. For in order to stand, each needs the support of many. Worse than the defense of evil is its protection, and even worse than the evil, the inability to hide it. The bequest of one vice is the bestowal of many others at interest. The wisest of persons may slip once but not twice, and that only by chance and not by design.

215

Pay attention to the one who works by indirection. It is a trick of the agent to put the will off guard that he may sneak up on it. For he who is outwitted is outdone. Such people conceal their intent only to attain it, and put it in the background in order that when they act it will be in the foreground: a shot that reaches its mark through its very carelessness. But attention should not be asleep when intent is so awake, and when this exits in order to deceive, let the other enter in order to undeceive. Let caution note the craftiness with which the person approaches, and recognize the pretexts advanced to arrive at a purpose. One thing is intended, another is pretended, and both are then skillfully turned about to hit the bull's-eye. Know, therefore, what you are conceding, and perhaps allow him to understand that you understand.

216

Be able to express yourself, not only clearly but with charm. Some conceive easily, but have a hard delivery. Yet without pains these children of the spirit, our thoughts and our judgments, are not rightly born. Others are like those vessels which hold much but yield little, while conversely others pour forth more than was anticipated. What resolution is to the will, exposition is to the mind. Both are great attributes. Clear heads are much praised, but those balmy may be venerated because not understood. Wherefore at times be not too clear, in order not to seem too ordinary. Yet how can a world get a concept of what it hears, if the speaker himself has no clear notion of what he is talking about?

217

Neither love nor hate without end. Confide in the friends of today as though the enemies of tomorrow, and the worst. And because such things come to pass, be prepared. Do not provide the deserters of friendship with the arms by which to make better war. Toward your enemies, on the other hand, keep open a door of reconciliation, and let it be a wide one, for that is safest. The thirst for vengeance yesterday becomes the torment of today, and the joy in revenge past resolves into remorse present.

218

Never act through obstinacy, but only through reason. Every obstinacy is a boil, the puss-filled daughter of passion, she who has never yet done anything right. There are those who reduce everything to war. Veritable highway robbers of friendly intercourse, they seek that all they push through be made a victory, and they know not peaceful pursuit. For command or for rule, such are pernicious, for they make edict of law, and foes of those who should be made their friends. They would arrange for their ends by intrigue, and attain them as the fruit of their craftiness. But when the great mass has dragged their duplicity into the open, it rises against them; it thwarts their plans and so they accomplish nothing. They go away loaded with trouble, and everyone adds to their burden. These people have crooked minds and

often accursed hearts. The way to treat these misbegotten is to flee
from them even to the Antipodes, for its crudeness is more tolerable
than their savageries.

219

Do not be thought a deceiver, though it is impossible to live today
without being one. Better prudent than crafty: To be smooth in your
way is to please everybody, but not everybody of your own house. Do
not let your sincerity degenerate into simple-mindedness, nor your
intelligence into trickery. Better be esteemed for your wisdom than
feared for your foxiness. The simple in heart are loved, even though
they are cheated. Let your greatest cunning lie in covering up what
looks like cunning. In the golden age it was simplicity that flourished;
in this, the iron age, it is duplicity. To have the name of a person who
knows what should be done, is honorable and inspires trust. But to
have that of being a sham, is disreputable and engenders mistrust.

220

When you can't wear the lion's skin, wear that of the fox. To know how
to yield to the times is to be ahead of them. He who accomplishes his
purpose never endangers his reputation. Where force fails, try art.
Travel over one road or another: either the highway of courage, or
the byway of cunning. More things have been gained by knack than by
knock. The wise have won much oftener than the valorous, and not
the other way around. When not possible to attain your end, register
your contempt for it.

221

Do not be a source of embarrassment either to yourself or to others.
There are people who offend the decencies, as much their own as
those of others, and always foolishly. They are met with easily and
parted from with difficulty. No day is complete for them without its
hundred annoyances; they have a humor for nothing, and so they
gainsay everybody and everything. They put on their understanding
wrong side out, and so find fault with everything. But the greatest
traducers of the mind are those who, unable to do anything right

themselves, call the efforts of all others wrong. Which explains why so many beasts roam the broad fields of the wild.

222

A self-controlled person evidences prudence. The tongue is a beast which once at large is hard to recapture and to chain. It is the pulse of the soul, from which the trained deduce its state; here the observant person feels the beat of the spirit. A sad fact that one who should be most restrained is often least so. A wiser person does not get stirred up or involved, thereby proving how much he is the master of himself. He goes carefully, a Janus in outlook, an Argus in discernment. It would have been better if Momus had cried for eyes in the hands instead of that little window in the breast.

223

Not too individual, either by affectation or through carelessness: Some individualize themselves by the craziness of their actions, but such had better be regarded as disgraces than as distinctions. Just as some stand out because of ugly face, these become known by the excrescences upon their deportment. These matters do not serve to make the individual, but only to mark him, and in very special fashion. For they merely move people at times to laughter, and at times to tears.

224

Know how to never take things against the grain, even though they come that way. Everything has its cutting and its blunt edge. The best and most useful of tools, if seized by the blade, wounds; while, on the contrary, the most destructive if grasped by the hilt, protects. Much that has given pain, if it had been taken rightly, would have given pleasure. For there is pleasure or pain in everything, and wisdom lies in hitting upon the profitable. For one and the same thing has very different faces, as seen in different lights. Look upon it in its happiest light, and do not get the controls mixed, as to what is good and what is bad. From this it comes that some discover satisfaction in everything, and others only grief. This is the great defense against the reverses of fortune, and a master rule of life, at all times and in all circumstances.

225

Know your chief weakness. No one lives without some counterweight even to his greatest gift, which when petted assumes tyranny. Start war upon it by calling out caution, and let your first move be a manifesto against it. For as soon as recognized, it may be conquered, especially if the victim sees as clearly as the onlookers. To be master of yourself, you must rise above yourself; bring this chief of your defects into subjection, and you finish off all the rest.

226

Be civil. Most neither speak nor act for what they are, but as they must. To persuade one of evil, anything will do, because slander is easily believed, however unbelievable. The most and the best of what is ours resides in the opinion of others. Some rest content because right is on their side; but this is not enough, for it needs the help of good form. To be obliging usually costs but little. Yet it is worth much, for with mere words you buy deeds. There is no bauble so mean in this great house of the world that once in the year it may not prove necessary, and however little its value, be missed if absent. Every person regards a subject as it affects him.

227

Not the victim of first impressions: Some people marry themselves to the first tale told, whence it follows that all others can only appear as concubines. And since the lie always pushes itself out in front, no room is left for the truth. But neither our wish for the first seen nor our sympathy for the first heard should thus be able to stuff us, for that marks a lack of capacity. Some people are like new casks which forever retain the smell of the first liquor poured into them, be it bad or good. When this shortsightedness comes to be known, it is fatal, for it makes room for malicious gossip, allowing those of evil intent to tinge the credulous with their color. Wherefore leave room always for a second impression. Alexander ever kept the other ear for the other side. Save space for the second and even the third report, for it argues small capacity to be too readily filled, and borders on the too passionate.

228

Do not be a scandal sheet. Much less, be held one, for it is to have the reputation of being a reputation killer. Do not be smart at the expense of another, which is more odious than difficult. All take vengeance upon such a one by speaking ill of him. And since he stands alone and they are many, he is conquered more quickly than they are convinced. Evil should never be our pleasure, and therefore not our theme. The slanderer is forever despised, and even when at times great persons are seen in his company, it is more because his mockery amuses them than because his wisdom enchants them. He who speaks evil will always have to hear still greater.

229

Know how to arrange your life with intelligence, and not as accident may determine, but with foresight and choice. It is a toilsome affair without recreation, like a long journey without inns; variety in mental equipment makes it happier. Spend the first period of beautiful life in conversation with the dead. We are born to know the world and to know ourselves, and the great books of truth make us persons. Let the second be spent with the living, to see and to know all the good that is upon this earth. For not everything is found in one country: The omnipresent Father has divided His blessings and has at times adorned the ugliest in the richest raiment. Let the third be wholly your own, for to live in the mind is the ultimate good fortune of a human being.

230

Open your eyes with time: Not all who see, see with open eyes, and not all who look, see. To see too late brings not help, but grief. Some start seeing when there is no longer anything to see, having sold off their house and substance before they ever came into them. It is a difficult matter to put understanding into one who has no will, and more difficult to put will into one who has no understanding. Those who comprehend play around such people as if they were blind, to everybody's amusement, and, because they are deaf of ear, they do not open their eyes to see. But there is no lack of people to encourage this blindness, for they live because the others do not. An unhappy nag, whose master has no eyes: She will run badly to fat.

231

Never show your work half-done. It can be enjoyed only when complete. All beginnings are without form, and the image of this shapelessness tarries in the imagination. The memory of the thing seen imperfect lingers into the completed, forbidding the enjoyment of the magnificent in one gaze. Even though this blurs the judgment of details, only through it is desire satisfied. Before an object is everything, it is nothing, and, in beginning to be, it is still very close to being nothing. The sight of preparation of even the daintiest morsel excites more to disgust than to appetite. Wherefore, let every great master look to it that his work be not seen in embryo, learning from nature herself not to bring it forth until it is ready to be seen.

232

Have just a touch of the commercial in you. Do not merely shop, but trade a little. Most philosophers are easy to cheat, for even though they know the unusual, they are ignorant of the usual of life, which is much more necessary. The contemplation of sublime affairs leaves them no time for thought of the mundane. And as they do not know the first thing about that which they ought to know, and about which all others can split hairs, they are either marveled at or considered fools by the ignorant of the common herd. Wherefore, let the person of wisdom see to it that he has a little of the commercial in him, just enough to keep him from being cheated, or even from being laughed at. Let him be a person fitted to the daily round, for even if this is not the highest thing in life, it is the most necessary. Of what use is knowledge unless it be made to function? And to know how to live today is the truest of sciences.

233

Do not fail to catch the other's mood, lest you give him pain instead of pleasure. With that by which some would oblige, they molest, because they do not grasp the spirit. Ways that flatter one, offend another, and what was intended as a compliment, becomes an affront. It has often cost more to make a person unhappy than it would have cost to make him happy. And so his gratitude and his thanks are lost, because the guiding star to his pleasure was not seen. For when you do not sense another's mood, it is hard to bring him satisfaction. Whence it comes that many in trying to voice a eulogy have pronounced a curse, and thus brought upon themselves a well-merited punishment; others think to charm by their eloquence, when they only bruise the spirit by their loquacity.

234

Never trust your honor to another without holding his in pawn. Proceed so that the advantage of silence or the danger of breaking it is mutual. In matters of honor the interests of the whole company must always be at stake; whence it comes that the name of one is guarded by each of the rest. Never trust your honor to another, but if you should at some time, let it be with all that art which is demanded when intelligence makes concession to caution. Let the risk be mutual and the need reciprocal, so that he who knows himself an accomplice will not convert himself into a witness against you.

235

Know how to beg. There is nothing more difficult for some, and nothing easier for others. There are those who do not know how to refuse: With such it is not necessary to be a burglar. There are others to whom "no" is always the first word and at any hour. With these, art is necessary and, with everybody, the right moment. Catch them in a happy mood, when recently refreshed in body or spirit, and when the attention of the patron has not already been awakened and has not foreseen the trick of the supplicant. The days of joy are the days in which favors are conferred, for they flow from the inside upon the outside. Do not approach when another has just been turned away, for at that moment all fear of saying "no" is gone. And after affliction is not a good time: Previously to have placed the other under obligation to you is to make the transaction merely a trade, provided of course that you are not dealing with a villain.

236

First make an obligation of what you are paid for afterwards. It is a trick of the political giants to yield favor before it is earned, for it betokens that the persons concerned are persons of honor. The favor thus advanced has double merit. For in the readiness with which it was bestowed, it lays greater obligation upon the one who receives it. And if later it is mere pay, given earlier it constitutes a promissory note. This is a subtle way of evening obligations, for what the one must do to discharge a debt, the other must do to discharge a duty. But this is true only between people with a sense of honor, for to mean-minded people, advance payment of a pledge acts more as a rein than as a spur.

237

Never participate in the secrets of those above you: You think to share the fruit, and you share the stones. Wherefore so many confidants die of want. They are bread sops, and run the risk of being eaten afterwards. The confidence of a prince is not a grant, but a tax. Many have broken the mirror that reminded them of their ugliness, and so we do not truly wish to see one who has seen us truly. Nor will we welcome one to whom we are unwelcome. Hold a whip hand too heavily over no one, least of all over the one in power. Let this be for favors bestowed, rather than for favors received, for the confidences of friendship are dangerous above all other things on earth. He who tells his secrets to another makes himself his slave, and this is a strain upon those who rule that cannot last. They will wish to regain their lost freedom, and to do so will trample upon everything, even justice. Secrets, therefore, should never be heard and never spoken.

238

Know the chink in your armor. Many would count as great persons, were it not that they lack something without which they can never attain the heights of being. It is obvious that many might be something much, if they could repair something little. Thus certain people lack earnestness, which blurs their great gifts. Others lack friendliness of disposition, a fault which those about them note all too quickly, especially in persons of position. Some want execution, and others, temper. All such frailties, if they were given heed, could easily be overcome, for a little care is able to impose upon the inborn a second nature.

239

Not too smart, for it is more important to be wise: To display too much edge is to go dull, for what is too pointed commonly breaks off. Most secure is the ordained truth; well to have fine brains, but not a babbling tongue. For too much discourse borders on dispute. Best is a good level judgment that does not wander afield more than may be necessary.

240

Know how to pretend ignorance. The wisest of persons may at times play this part, for there are many occasions when the better wisdom consists in showing that you have none. Do not be ignorant, but deport yourself as though ignorant. Of little importance to be intelligent with the ignoramuses, or to have a mind among the witless. Wherefore be able to speak to every person in his own language. The fool is not the one who affects foolishness, but the one who is affected of it. The simpleton is the one who cannot double in the part, for to this extremity has trickery driven us. In order to be welcome, the only way is to come clothed in the skin of the simplest of the brutes.

241

Know how to take jokes, but do not play them. The first is a kind of gallantry; the second a way into difficulty. One who grows ill-humored at the fiesta has much of a beast in him, and shows himself a greater. A good joke enlivens, and to know how to take it shows good sense. Let one who is piqued show no irritation toward the one who piqued him. Better yet, take no notice, and safest of all, let it pass. For what is most serious has always sprung from what was most silly. There is nothing that demands greater caution and greater skill: Before you begin, know exactly to what point of sufferance the soul of your subject may be driven.

242

Pursue your advantage. Some spend everything in getting started and so never get anywhere. They plan but they do not build. It is the mark of a vacillating spirit never to become distinguished, because nothing is followed through, but everything is left to itself, even when well conceived. In others it is the mark of impatience of the spirit: a failing of the Spaniards, just as patience is the virtue of the Belgians. They finish things as the others are finished by them. Some sweat to conquer a difficulty, only to rest content in their labors, not knowing how to bring victory home. Which proves that they can but that they do not care. But this is really only evidence of incapacity or of frivolousness. If the undertaking was good, why was it not finished? Or if bad, why was it begun? Let sagacity retrieve its prey and not be content only to drive it from cover.

243

Not always the innocent: Let the subtlety of the snake alternate with the simplicity of the dove. Nobody is easier to cheat than an honest person. One who never lies believes readily, and one who never cheats trusts readily. To be cheated does not always evidence stupidity, but often goodness. Two kinds of people know well how to avoid hurt: the experienced, at their great cost; and the crafty, at the great cost of others. Here let intelligence show itself as able to disentangle, as craftiness is able to entangle. Let no one seek to be a person so honest as to give opportunity to the other to be dishonest. Be a cross of the dove with the snake; not a monster, but a marvel.

244

Know how to engender obligation. Some can make a favor received look like a favor bestowed; it appears, or they make it appear, that they made payment when they received it. There are people so ingenious that they can turn what is to their advantage into what looks like opportunity for the other. By such trick they turn matters about so that it seems as though the other had been done a service when actually he gave it. Managing with extravagant politeness to reverse the order of the obligation, or at least making it doubtful who gained the profit from whom, they have bought at the price of fine words the better bargain. Through their exhibition of pleasure in something, they create also a sense of thankfulness and satisfaction. They invoke courtesy to make an indebtedness out of what was given them. By this trick they change a passive obligation into an active one, thus proving themselves better politicians than grammarians. A great game this, but a greater that of understanding it and reversing the nonsense by restoring to each the honor due, recovering for everyone what is rightfully theirs.

245

Talk always about the singular and forego the common. It enriches argument. Do not hold in too high opinion the person who never opposes you, for that is not a token of love for you, but of love for himself. Do not allow yourself to be deceived through flattery or be pleased by it, but cast it from you. Always hold it to your credit that some speak against you, especially if it be those who speak ill of all that is best. Pity the one whose ways please everybody, because it is a sign that they are of no value, since excellence belongs to the few.

246

Never explain unless asked. Even when asked, it is a crime if over-done. To excuse yourself before occasion demands is to accuse yourself. And to allow yourself to be bled in health is to make eyes at disease and at malice. To explain in advance is to awaken slumbering doubt. A person of sense will never show notice of another's suspicion, for that is to go hunting for trouble. Then is the time to give it the lie through what is the uprightness of your whole way of life.

247

Enjoy a little more and strive a little less. Others argue to the contrary, but happy leisure is worth more than drive. For nothing belongs to us except time, wherein even the homeless dwell. Equally infelicitous to squander precious existence in stupid drudgery, as in an excess of noble business. Be not crushed under success, in order not to be crushed under envy. It is to trample upon life and to suffocate the spirit. Some would include knowledge here, but one who is without knowledge is without life.

248

Do not let the latest thing carry you away. Some listen constantly for the latest news, which makes them go to ridiculous extremes. For they are as soft and as impressionable as wax, and therefore always carry the seal of the last signet, which has already stamped all the preceding. People like that never stay put, because they are so mobile they constantly change color. They are bad as confidants, children all their lives, and like them ever changing in spirit and feelings. Perpetually in a state of flux, and always halt in will and in judgment, they wobble first to the one side and then to the other.

249

Do not begin to live where life should end. Some take to rest at its beginning and leave labor for its end. The essential should be first, and then, if chance is left, the accessory. Others seek to triumph before they have battled. And some begin by study of the trivial, postponing those studies which might bring them fame and success until the evening of life. Another has gone dizzy before the climb toward fortune has begun. A knowledge of values is all-important, in order to learn and be able to live.

250

When must the opposite be inferred? Whenever we are addressed by malice. With some everything must be turned about, for their yes means no, and their no means yes. When they decry anything, they have a high regard for it, for one who would gain something for himself will cheapen it before others. Not all praise is meant well, for some praise the evil in order not to praise the good. And to one to whom nothing is bad, nothing will be good either.

251

Employ human means as though there were no divine, and divine means as though there were no human. These are the rules of the Great Master, and to them no comment need be added.

252

Neither wholly yours nor wholly another's: Each is a vulgar tyranny. From wishing everything to oneself, it follows that one must shortly want the whole world. People of this stripe do not know how to yield the smallest point, or how to sacrifice an atom of their profit. Feeling no obligation, they trust luck, and this support commonly fails them. Well at times to be dependent upon others, that the others may be dependent upon you. One who holds a public office must be a public slave, else let him renounce his crown with his cargo, as said the old lady to Hadrian. On the other side stand those who belong too completely to others, for stupidity always goes to extremes, and in this instance most unhappily. For not a day, not even an hour, remains their own, bound over so entirely that one such has been called the man for everybody. This extends even unto their attitude, for they think only of everybody and never of themselves. Let the person of sense realize that none is looking out for him, but only has selfish interest in him or through him.

253

Good to be a bit vague: Most people have low regard for what they understand, and venerate only what is beyond them. The things that they treasure must have cost them something, wherefore they honor most what they cannot grasp. Always appear a little wiser and smarter than may be demanded by one with whom you deal, to command respect, but properly and not excessively. Even though it be true that with persons of understanding, wisdom counts for everything, for the majority some kind of oratory is still necessary. This in order not to give them time for criticism, by keeping them busy with the mere business of interpretation. Many praise, but if asked can give no reason. Why? For they revere all that is hidden because mysterious, and they sing its praises because they hear its praises sung.

254

Do not scorn an evil because it is small. Evil never comes alone. It always comes in battalions, as does joy. Good fortune and bad concentrate where they are already thick, and it is the rule that all flee the unfortunate and tie up with the fortunate. Even the doves, with all their simplicity, bow in homage to their most white. Everything fails the unlucky: herself, her reason, and her guiding star. Never awaken misfortune when she sleeps. A slip is little, but to have this followed by a fall is fatal, for you do not know how far that will carry you. Just as nothing that is good seems ever to come to fulfillment, so nothing that is bad seems ever to come to an end. Against that which is sent us from heaven, show patience; against that which springs from this earth, intelligence.

255

Know how to do good: Little, and often. Never allow the obligation to exceed what can be repaid; for one who grants too much, no longer grants but sells. Neither must the well of gratefulness be drained, for when it is seen that a *quid pro quo* is impossible, a friendship is done. Nothing more is necessary to lose most friends than to place them in too heavy debt. For in order not to pay, they take themselves off, and from vassals turn into enemies. The idol does not care to be faced by the sculptor who made it, nor the debtor by the benefactor. Clever in giving, to bestow what costs little but is wanted much, that it be cherished more.

256

Go prepared, always, against the discourteous, the stubborn, the presumptuous, and every manner of fool. There are many, and sanity consists in not being with them. Arm yourself daily with resolution on this point, before the mirror of your watchfulness, and thus be provided against foolish accident. Go ready for the unexpected, never exposing public estimate of you to mere contingency. The person forearmed with intelligence will not be engaged by impertinence. The way is difficult through this human sea, for it is filled with rocks upon which standing founders. To sail around them is safest, if counsel be taken from Ulysses. Of great value in all these matters is a feigned blindness; cover everything with the cloak of courtesy, for that is the quiet way out of all embarrassments.

257

Never arrive at open rupture, for that is to come off with a wounded reputation. Every person counts as an enemy, but not everyone as a friend. Few can do us good, but nearly all, harm. From the day he has broken with a beetle, the eagle no longer dwells securely even in the lap of Jupiter. Hypocrites with open claw stir up the fire against you which has been smoldering in the hope of this opportunity. And from friends now spoiled, there emerge the worst of enemies. Each charges the other with faults that are his own, while of those who look on, each speaks as he feels and feels as he wishes to feel. But all pronounce you guilty, because in the beginning you lacked prudence, in the end, patience, and at all times common sense. When a parting of the ways must come, find an excuse for it. Let it be rather a growing coolness between friends than a mounting fury between enemies. That old saying about a good retirement fits here.

258

Discover someone to help shoulder your misfortunes. Then you will never be alone, and even in the hour of danger, not freighted with all the distress. Some think to carry off all the applause, and end by carrying off all the hisses. In such circumstance have at hand a confidant to make excuse for you, or to aid you in bearing the evil. Neither fate nor the crowd so readily attacks two. Which explains why the intelligent physician, having missed the cure, does not miss calling another, who under the name of consultant helps carry the coffin. Divide with another your burdens and your sorrows, for misfortune is doubly unbearable to one who stands alone.

259

Foresee insult and make of it compliment, for it is cleverer to avoid insult than to avenge it. It is a great trick to make a friend of one who wished to be a rival, and to turn into a protector of your honor one who threatened its injury. It helps to know how to place one under obligation; time for insult is taken from the one who must fill it with thanksgiving. It is to know how to live to be able to convert into pleasure what was to have been pain: Transform into trust malevolence itself.

260

Neither be all nor give all to anyone: Neither blood nor friendship nor the most pressing obligation justifies it. For there is a big difference between the bestowal of your affection and the bestowal of yourself. The closest of ties must still admit of exceptions, and not on this account give offense to the laws of intimacy. For something should always be kept hidden even from a friend, and something concealed even from a father by his son. Certain secrets are kept from the one and imparted to the other, and vice versa. Wherefore it may be said that everything is revealed or that everything is concealed, depending upon whom one is with.

261

Do not persist in folly. Some make a duty of failure and having started down the wrong road, think it a badge of character to continue. They accuse themselves of error before the bar of their inner selves, but before the bar of the outer world they excuse themselves. Thus if at the start of their unwisdom they were marked imprudent, in its prosecution they are marked fools. Neither rash promise nor wrong resolve lays obligation upon any person. Yet some will on this account continue in their sulkiness and carry on in their contrariness, wishing to be known as constant in their idiocies.

262

Know how to forget: It is more luck than art. Matters best forgotten are those best remembered, for memory plays the villain by forsaking us when we need her most, and the clown by appearing when we would see her least. In all that gives pain she is most lavish, and in all that might give joy, most negligent. At times the only remedy for an evil lies in forgetting it, and to be able to forget is the remedy. Wherefore train your memory to these comfortable manners, for she can bring you heaven or hell. Those self-satisfied are of course excepted, for in their state of innocence they are already rejoicing in the happy state of feeblemindedness.

263

Many of the things that bring delight should not be owned. They are more enjoyed if another's than if yours. The first day they give pleasure to the owner, but in all the rest to the others. What belongs to another rejoices doubly, because without the risk of going stale, and with the satisfaction of freshness. Everything tastes better after fasting, even the drink from another being judged nectar. The possession of things not only diminishes their enjoyment but augments their annoyance. This whether shared or not shared, for they are only held in stewardship and attract many more as enemies than as friends.

264

No days unalert: Fate likes to play the buffoon and to upset everything unawares in order to catch the sleeping. Always stand ready for inspection in spirit, in mind, in fortitude, even in appearance. For the day that these are left to themselves becomes the day of their downfall. Alertness when most necessary is always missing, and not to give the matter a thought is to be slated for destruction. It has always been the strategy of another's watchfulness to call out your qualifications for most rigorous inspection when in undress. The days for the parade are already known and may be discounted; but on the day least expected, she orders them up for review to test their real worth.

265

Know how to put fire into your subordinates. The need to act on occasion has made giants of many, just as the danger of drowning has made swimmers. Under such circumstances many have discovered a courage and even a capacity which would have remained buried in their faintheartedness if the emergency had not arisen. In danger lies the opportunity for fame, wherefore a nobleman who sees his honor threatened has the energy of a thousand. Queen Isabela the Catholic knew and knew well this law, as she knew all the others, of laying responsibility upon her subjects. And it was to such politic favor that the Great Captain owed his name, and many others their eternal glory. People are made great through such challenge.

266

Do not become insipid by being too sweet, for such is the one who never becomes outraged. Those so insentient are hardly human. Not always is this born of laziness, but of incapacity. Proper feeling upon occasion marks the person, for the birds soon amuse themselves of a scarecrow. To let the acrid alternate with the sweet, is proof of good taste; the sweet alone is for children and fools. It is a grave disease to be reduced through pure goodness to this state of feeling nothing.

267

Soft words with tenderness of heart for thorns pierce the body, but hard words pierce the spirit. A good cake gives good odor to the breath; a great trick in life to know how to sell the air. Most things are paid for in words, and they suffice to discharge the impossible debt. Heavenly business is done with the heavens, and life-giving words give life. Always carry the mouth full of sugar to sweeten the speech, that it may be found good even to your enemies. For the only way to be loved is to be lovable.

268

A wise person does at once what a fool does at last. Both do the same thing, only at different times: the first in season and the second out. One who starts with understanding inside out must continue in this style ever afterwards: wearing about his feet what he should have placed upon his head, making left of what is right, and so proceeding in everything he does. There is only one good way to bring him to account, and that is to make him do by compulsion what he should have done through desire. But the person of sense sees at once what sooner or later must be, and does it to his joy and to his credit.

269

Capitalize your novelty; for as long as you are deemed new, you rate high. The novel stands well everywhere because it is different. It refreshes the taste, wherefore the brand-new mediocrity is more cherished than the shopworn perfection. The best of things grow grubby and become old; only note that this glory of the new is short-lived, and that in four days respect for it will fade. Know therefore how to make use of these first days of approval, how to catch this acclaim in its flight and seize all that is justly yours. For when the fire of the new is spent, ardor cools, and the excitement for the young will have to be exchanged for the boredom of the old. Believe then that all that is yours also has its day and that it passes.

270

Do not alone condemn what pleases the many. To be so satisfying to the public, it must contain some good which, even though it cannot be explained, must bring joy. The person who stands apart is always suspect, and when wrong becomes ridiculous. Your action serves more to discredit your judgment than the object, and so you are likely to be left alone in your bad taste. If you do not know how to strike upon the good, conceal your blindness. And do not condemn wholesale, for bad choice is ordinarily the child of ignorance. What all say is either so or wished so.

271

Let the one who knows little play safe. In every profession, though not judged smart, one who plays it safe will be judged sound. One who knows much may take a chance and let his imagination roam; but one who knows little and takes chances voluntarily tries suicide. Hold always to the right, for what is established as right cannot be wrong: The king's highway is fixed for the simpleton. This law for everybody, the one who knows much and the one who knows little: There is better sense in safety than in singularity.

272

Sell your stuff at the price of courtesy, for that imposes the heaviest obligation. Never can the demand of a dealer raise the price to what is paid freely by the satisfied customer. Courtesy not only pays but it pledges, and it is gallant manner that imposes the greatest obligation. Nothing costs a person of conscience more than a gift, for it is sold twice and at a double price: that of its own value, and that of politeness. Nevertheless it remains true that to people of mean spirit such noble talk is mere gibberish, for they do not understand the idioms of good style.

273

Understand the spirit of those with whom you deal, in order to grasp their intent. For if the cause is well-understood, the effect is known; and from the first, the motive for the second. The melancholic perpetually augurs disaster, and the defamer, crime. In either instance the worst of what may be in the offing, for unable to encompass the existent good, each forecasts the possible evil. The person of passion always speaks of matters far differently from what they are, for he uses the terms of passion and not those of reason. Thus does everyone babble according to his feelings or his mood, and all very far from the truth. Know how to read a face and to decipher a soul from its lineaments. Hold him who laughs ceaselessly as fool, and him who never laughs as false. Be on guard against the inquisitor, either because he is frivolous or a spy. Expect little good of people misborn, for they are given to revenging themselves upon nature; as she showed little regard for them, they show little regard for her. Even so does a person tend to be the fool as he is fair of face.

274

Have something attractive about you, for its is the magic of civil intercourse. Use this smooth hook more to catch goodwill than good things, but always use it. Merit is not enough if it is not made to count through opportunity, for this is what brings forth acclaim. To have the cut is to carry the best scepter of rule, which even though most a matter of luck, can be helped by art. For where the ground is already rich, fertilization aids most. By such means popular yearning is created until all hearts are won.

275

Join in, but not indecently. Not always the lead, and not always the clown; this is gallant. Some concession may be made to decorum to gain popularity; at times go as far as the crowd goes but without becoming indecent. For one who is counted the fool in public will not be voted the sage in secret. More may be lost in one day of foolery than can be regained in a whole age of seriousness. But on this account do not forever stand apart, for to be thus singular is to condemn the others. Much less act the prude, leaving this to its own sex, for even the too pious are ridiculous. The best a man can do is to appear the man, for a woman may play the man to perfection but not the other way about.

276

Know how to refresh the spirit through nature and through art. Once in every seven years, so they say, we are made over. Let it mark an elevation and realization of the better spirit. With the first seven years the intelligence enters; with each succeeding seven let some new virtue shine forth. Take note of this natural change in order to help it along, forever looking toward the improvement of all. In this way many have changed their deportment with change in social status or their business. At times it goes unnoticed until the alteration has become excessive. At twenty-one is a peacock, at thirty a lion, at forty a camel, at fifty a snake, at sixty a dog, at seventy an ape, and at eighty, nothing.

277

A person of show: Show is the spotlight for the talents. There is a moment for every one of them: Seize it, for not every day will be its day of triumph. There are knights in armor of which even a little shines forth and much bedazzles. When now to their great gifts is added an ability to display them, these people pass as prodigies. There are nations that know how to put on, and it is Spain that does it superlatively. It was light that first revealed the whole of creation, and it is show that satisfies, supplying much and giving second life to everything, especially when joined to reality. The heavens from which springs every perfect thing give to each its perfect setting, for either without the other would be sacrilege. But exhibition requires art. Even that which is most excellent leans upon its surroundings, and every day is not its day. Show fares badly when out of season. For no attribute demands greater freedom from affectation, upon which it perishes because so close to vanity and this to cheapness. All ostentation must be much tempered that it descend not to the vulgar, for by the understanding its excess is discredited. It reveals itself best perhaps in a silent eloquence, in a careless revelation of some high quality. Wise concealment makes the most effective of parades, because such secrecy most piques curiosity into life. A great trick not to exhibit all you have at once, but to allow frequent peeps, always bringing forward more. For one accomplishment must be the pledge of another and a greater, and the applause for the first, a welcome to those to follow.

278

Avoid all badges. For when they serve to mark you, even your distinctions become defects. All are the awards of peculiarity, which always raises question: for the singular is left to itself. Even beauty, when too surpassing, is discredited. Whatever attracts notice gives offense, especially in matters already of bad repute. But some seek prominence in vice itself, hunting for distinction in villainy in order so to assure themselves an infamous notoriety. Even judgment, when too refined, degenerates into babble.

279

Do not argue with an arguer. You must decide whether the argument springs from astuteness or vulgarity. It is not always pigheadedness but may be a trick. Pay heed therefore not to entangle yourself in the one while disentangling yourself from the other. No precaution more in order when with spies; and against the lock-pickers of the soul, no better countertrick than to leave the key of caution inside the door.

280

A person of principle: Right dealing is finished; truth is held the liar; good friends are few; for the best of service, the worst of pay; and this is the style the world over today. Whole nations are committed to evil dealings. With one you fear insecurity; with another, inconstancy; with a third, treason. Wherefore let this bad faith of others serve you, not as example but as warning. The peril of the situation lies in the unhinging of your own integrity at the sight of such baseness in conduct. But the person of principle never forgets what he is, because of what others are.

281

The grace of those who understand: More to be cherished is the soft yes of one person than the cheers of a whole crowd. The belch of the obstinate is not elevating. The sages speak with understanding, wherefore their praise brings lifelong satisfaction. Wise Antigonus reduced the whole theater of his fame to one Zeno, and Plato called Aristotle his whole school. Some heed only to fill their stomachs, albeit with the worst of rubbish. Even the rulers need the grace of biographers, and they fear their pens more than ugly women fear a painter's brush.

<h2 style="text-align:center">282</h2>

Use your absence to increase the respect and the honor in which you are held. If presence serves to diminish glory, absence serves to increase it. One who when absent was counted a lion, when present was counted ridiculous and as something the mountain brought forth. The greatest gifts lose their luster when handled, for it is easier to see the husk than the rich interior of a spirit. The imagination goes far beyond what is glimpsed, and fraud, which commonly enters through the ears, has a way of going out through the eyes. One who keeps himself in the halfway place of public opinion regarding himself keeps his reputation. Even the Phoenix makes capital of its absence in order to plume itself, and of the cry for it in order to gain acclaim.

<h2 style="text-align:center">283</h2>

A person of inventive mind: It marks the greatest genius, yet who can be such without a grain of dementia? Inventiveness springs from genius, good choice from the intelligence. The former is a gift from heaven and most rare, but the capacity to choose right is given to many. The talent for discovery is vouchsafed to very few, and only to the first in their line or in time. The new gives joy, and when of happy turn it puts a double halo upon the good. In matters of judgment it is dangerous, for seemingly paradoxical; but in matters of genius, it is laudable, and when either succeeds deserving of all praise.

<h2 style="text-align:center">284</h2>

Be not obtrusive, and so not slighted. Have respect for yourself, if you would be respected. Better pull than push. Arrive wanted in order to arrive welcomed. Never to come without being invited is to leave without being sent. One reaps all the indignation, who plows ahead alone, if the thing goes badly, and none of the thanks if it goes well. The too obstinate is the lowest of the low, and because he pushes himself in with effrontery, he is pushed out in confusion.

285

Do not die of another's misery. Beware of one who is stuck in the mud, and note that he calls to you, to be comforted by your mutual unhappiness. These people are on the hunt for those who will help them carry their misfortune. And of those to whom in their prosperity they gave the cold shoulder, they today ask the hand. Great coolness is necessary with the drowning, if you would bring them help without peril to yourself.

286

Not beholden for everything or to everybody, for that is to be a slave, and a common slave: Some are born luckier than others; the one to do more good, the other to receive it better. Independence is more precious than any gift for which you might forfeit it. More satisfying far, that many depend upon you than that you depend upon anybody. The power to command has only one advantage: the power to do greater good. But be most careful not to mistake an obligation put upon you for a favor, because usually the other's astuteness has so managed that it will so appear.

287

Do nothing in passion or everything goes wrong. He who is not in command of himself cannot work for himself. Passion invariably banishes reason. Here have recourse to another more prudent, who may be anyone, provided unimpassioned. They who look on always see more than those who are in the play, for they are not excited. As quickly as you discover yourself roused, let intelligence blow the retreat. For the blood has hardly rushed into the head before all you do shows blood. In one brief moment is spewed forth the substance of many days of shame for you and of slander for another.

288

Live as circumstance permits. All rule, all converse, everything must be determined by the contingency. Wish for what offers, for time and tide wait for no one. Do not journey through life by statute, even when such has the face of virtue, or indicate in terms too precise what alone will satisfy you. For tomorrow you may have to drink of the water that you disdained today. There are some so perverse that they would have every circumstance of life fit itself to their vagaries and not the other way about. The person of wisdom knows better that prudence consists in behaving according to the circumstance.

289

The greatest human defect, to give sign of being human: For one ceases to be held divine from the day that he lets himself be seen human. Witlessness is the great head wind to renown. Just as the discreet person is held to be more than human, so the lightheaded is held to be less. There is no shortcoming that cheapens more, for frivolousness stands directly opposed to earnestness. A fool can never prove himself a person of substance, especially if an old fool, when his years require that he have sense. And though this fault is the fault of many, it cannot be denied that it is peculiarly degrading.

290

A rare joy, to couple esteem with affection: But be not too much loved, if you would maintain the respect in which you are held. Love is bolder than hatred, and affection and veneration do not marry well. Even though you may not be too much feared, you may not be too much loved either. Affection ushers in familiarity, and for every step she takes forward, respect takes one backward. Better to be loved appreciatively than devotedly, for that is the love more befitting the great.

291

Know how to analyze a person. The alertness of the examiner is matched against the reserve of the examined. But great judgment is called for to take the measure of another. More important far to know the composition and the properties of people than those of herbs and stones. This is the most delicate of the occupations of life, for the metals are known by their ring, and people by what they speak. Words reveal the mind; and more, the mind's workings. To this end the greatest caution is necessary, and the clearest observation, the subtlest understanding, and the most critical judgment.

292

Your gifts must be greater than your work requires, and not the other way around. For however high may be your post, you in your person must show yourself superior to it. A person of great qualifications tends to grow, and to show this increasingly in his work. But the person of mean heart atrophies and soon reaches the end, both of his duties and his reputation. Great Augustus held himself greater as person than as prince, to which end greatness of spirit avails much, and yet more an intelligent self-confidence.

293

Be mature. It gives radiance to the person, yet more to the personality. For as material weight makes gold precious, moral weight enhances the person. It is the halo about every talent and the reason for its veneration. The composure of a man is the façade of his spirit. This is not an old fool with the palsy, as silly humor would have it, but one with an authority most serene. He speaks with finality and acts with certainty. It is the picture of the complete person. For each is considered a person to the extent he has matured, and he began to be mature and to carry authority when he ceased to be a child.

294

Be moderate in opinion. Everyone believes what suits his interests, and he is filled with excuses for his stand. For in most instances judgment gives way to feeling. Thus two opinions confront each other and each believes that his is the side of reason. But she, always most fair, cannot be two-faced. The person of sense goes cautiously in so delicate a situation; misgivings in his own mind moderate his judgment regarding that of another. At such moment let him imagine himself placed on the other side and examine the arguments from there. He will not then utterly damn the other, nor yet justify himself entirely in what is so puzzling.

295

Not a braggart, but a doer: They make the greatest show of what they have done, who have done least. Everything is made to appear marvelous and in the silliest fashion. Veritable chameleons for applause, they give everyone their fill of laughter. Conceit is always frowned upon, but here it is ridiculed. These ants of honor go collecting like beggars. But real achievement needs no such affectation. Rest in accomplishment and leave talk to others. Do, and do not brag. Nor with gold rent yourself a pen, for such writes dirt that sickens the knowing. Aspire to be heroic, not only to seem it.

296

A person of quality and of bearing: The first-rate makes the first-rate person, and one of these counts more than a thousand of the mediocre. There was one who was pleased that all he had was big, even to the kitchenware; how much more should the great person strive that the gifts of his spirit be such. Everything is infinite, everything immeasurable in God; and so must everything about a hero be great, and majestic. Wherefrom it comes that all his acts and even his thinking go clothed in one transcendent glory.

297

Deal always as though seen. The seeing person is the one who sees that he is seen or will be seen. He knows that the walls have ears, and that what is evil breaks its fetters to be free. Even when alone, he works as though the eyes of the world were upon him, because he knows that everything comes to be known. He holds as witnesses today those who will be such tomorrow because of what was disclosed to them. The only person unconcerned with what might be seen in his house from that of another, is he who would have the whole world look in.

298

Three things make the prodigy, and they are the greatest gifts of divine generosity: a fertile mind, a deep understanding, and a cultivated taste. A great advantage to have a good imagination, but a greater, to be able to think straight. To have a mind for what is good! Genius should not have its being in the spine, where it would be more steady than ready. Straight thinking is the fruit of reason. At twenty years desire rules us; at thirty, expediency; at forty, judgment. There are minds that radiate light like the eyes of the lynx, which in the greatest darkness see most clearly. Then there are those born for the occasion, who always strike upon what is most fitting. Much awaits them, and a well-blessed harvest. But good taste lends flavor to all of life.

299

Leave hunger unsated: The cup must be torn from the lips even with its nectar. Desire is the measure of value, wherefore it is the trick of good taste even for the thirst of the body, to satisfy but not to sate. The good, when small, is doubly good. Great is the fall upon second appearance. A surfeit of what is most pleasing is dangerous, for it cheapens eternal quality itself. The only way to please your host is to leave with an appetite still stimulated by a hunger still retained. If hurt must be felt, let it be that of a desire unsatisfied, rather than that of hunger gratified. Happiness suffered for is doubly sweet.

300

In one word: A saint. For that is to say everything at once. For virtue is the bond of all the perfections, and the heart of all life's satisfactions. It makes a person sensible, alert, farseeing, understanding, wise, courageous, considerate, upright, joyous, welcomed, truthful, and a universal idol. And three are the S's that make for happiness: saintliness, sanity, and sapience. Virtue is the sun of our lesser world, the sky over which is a good conscience. It is so beautiful that it finds favor of God and of humankind. There is nothing lovely without virtue, and nothing hateful without vice. For virtue is the essence of wisdom, and all else is folly. Capacity and greatness must be measured in terms of virtue and not in those of fortune. Virtue alone is sufficient unto itself. And it, only, makes a person worth loving in life, and in death, worth remembering.

SUGGESTED READING

BRAUDEL, FERDINAND. *Civilization and Capitalism, Volume 2, The Wheels of Commerce.* Trans. Sian Reynolds. Berkeley: University of California Press, 1992.

GREENBLATT, STEPHEN. *Renaissance Self-Fashioning, From More to Shakespeare.* Chicago: University of Chicago Press, 1980.

HABERMAS, JÜRGEN. *The Structural Transformation of the Public Sphere: An Inquiry into a Category of Bourgeois Society.* Trans. Thomas Burger. Cambridge, MA: MIT Press, 1991.

IFE, B. W. *Reading and Fiction in Golden Age Spain: A Platonist Critique and Some Picaresque Replies.* Cambridge, UK: Cambridge University Press, 1985.

KASSIER, THEODORE L. *The Truth Disguised, Allegorical Structure and Technique in Gracián's* Criticón. London: Tamesis, 1976.

LACOUTURE, JEAN. *Jesuits: A Multibiography.* Trans. Jeremy Leggatt. Washington DC: Counterpoint, 1995.

MOTTOLA, ANTHONY, TRANS. *The Spiritual Exercises of St. Ignatius.* New York: Doubleday, 1964.

Look for the following titles, available now from
The Barnes & Noble Library of Essential Reading.

Visit your Barnes & Noble bookstore,
or shop online at *www.bn.com/loer*

Treatise of Human Nature, A	David Hume	0760771723
Trial and Death of Socrates, The	Plato	0760762007
Twelve Years a Slave	Solomon Northup	0760783349
Up From Slavery	Booker T. Washington	0760752346
Utilitarianism	John Stuart Mill	0760771758
Vindication of the Rights of Woman, A	Mary Wollstonecraft	0760754942
Voyage of the *Beagle*, The	Charles Darwin	0760754969
Wealth of Nations, The	Adam Smith	0760757615
Wilderness Hunter, The	Theodore Roosevelt	0760756031
Will to Believe and Human Immortality, The	William James	0760770190
Will to Power, The	Friedrich Nietzsche	0760777772
Worst Journey in the World, The	Aspley Cherry-Garrard	0760757593

FICTION AND LITERATURE

Abbott, Edwin A.	Flatland	0760755876
Austen, Jane	Love and Freindship	0760768560
Braddon, Mary Elizabeth	Lady Audley's Secret	0760763046
Bronte, Charlotte	Professor, The	0760768854
Burroughs, Edgar Rice	Land that Time Forgot, The	0760768862
Burroughs, Edgar Rice	Martian Tales Trilogy, The	076075585X
Butler, Samuel	Way of All Flesh, The	0760765855
Castiglione, Baldesar	Book of the Courtier, The	0760768323
Cather, Willa	Alexander's Bridge	0760768870
Cather, Willa	One of Ours	0760777683
Chaucer, Geoffrey	Troilus and Criseyde	0760768919
Chesterton, G. K.	Ball and the Cross, The	0760783284
Chesterton, G. K.	Innocence and Wisdom of Father Brown, The	0760773556
Chesterton, G. K.	Man Who Was Thursday, The	0760763100
Childers, Erskine	Riddle of the Sands, The	0760765235
Cleland, John	Fanny Hill	076076591X
Conrad, Joseph	Secret Agent, The	0760783217
Cooper, James Fenimore	Pioneers, The	0760779015
Cummings, E. E.	Enormous Room, The	076077904X
Defoe, Daniel	Journal of the Plague Year, A	0760752370
Dos Passos, John	Three Soldiers	0760757542
Doyle, Arthur Conan	Complete Brigadier Gerard, The	0760768897
Doyle, Arthur Conan	Lost World, The	0760755833
Doyle, Arthur Conan	White Company and Sir Nigel, The	0760768900

THE BARNES & NOBLE
LIBRARY OF ESSENTIAL READING

This series has been established to provide affordable access to books of literary, academic, and historic value—works of both well-known writers and those who deserve to be rediscovered. Selected and introduced by scholars and specialists with an intimate knowledge of the works, these volumes present complete, original texts in a modern, readable typeface—welcoming a new generation of readers to influential and important books of the past. With more than 300 titles already in print and more than 100 forthcoming, the Library of Essential Reading offers an unrivaled variety of thought, scholarship, and entertainment. Best of all, these handsome and durable paperbacks are priced to be exceptionally affordable. For a full list of titles, visit *www.bn.com/loer*.